A Thousand Paths to Hope

A Thousand Paths to
hope

Jane Garton

Contents

Introduction 6

Staying Hopeful 8

Hope at Work 66

Hope and Relationships 130

Living Hopefully 178

What is Hope? 242

Spiritual Hope 290

The Hopeful Personality 354

Words of Hope 402

Introduction

In a world beset by ever more new threats—terrorism, eco-disaster, and epidemics—it can be hard to find a reason for hope. In fact it is these very threats that make hope more vital than ever before. Our leaders need hope to drive government; and at a personal level hope is what gives us a reason to carry on.

But what is this thing called hope? And how can we cultivate it? Is it merely a delusion—"pie in the sky when you die"—that blinds us to the harsh realities of everyday life? As the philosopher Voltaire said, "One day everything will be well, that is our hope. Today everything is fine, that is our illusion." Or is hope an essential ingredient of our lives, the thing that enables us to face life's challenges positively, taking risks and making the most of a situation however bad the circumstances?

The truth is when the going gets tough—in our own life or in the bigger context of the worldwide stage—hope can turn disaster into triumph. In the pages that follow, you will learn how you can achieve this quality we call hopefulness. To do so requires courage, strength, and imagination. If this book helps you on your journey it will have achieved what it set out to do. We hope it does.

Staying Hopeful

The darkest hour is just before dawn. Never give up hope.

However dark the sky, the stars are still there.

Bad times will pass;
night comes before sunrise.

Better to light a candle than complain about the dark.

Life is too short to live in the dark
—step into the sun with hope.

Never dread the winter; rather, hope for spring.

No sunrise finds us where sunset left us.

Kahlil Gibran

Hope is the feeling that how you are feeling isn't permanent.

Where there is a will, there is a way.

Nightmares can be conquered with dreams.

**From conflicts
new ideas
are born.**

**Hope is all around you;
every cloud has a silver lining.**

No matter how hard life may seem, the most important thing is to live it with hope.

A life without hope is a life without possibilities.

Hope is always waiting for you. If you feel defeated, all you have to do is ask for hope and it will appear.

Hope never leaves you, you leave it.

Hope is important because it can make the here and now less difficult.

Hoping that things will be better tomorrow can make the hardships of today easier to bear.

Believe in yourself and know that you will feel hopeful again.

Think negatively and your life will spiral into depression.

To give up hope is to give up on life.

Life is in the hoping. The process of life keeps happening.

Hope transforms poison into crystal-clear waters.

No matter how dismal things may seem, if you search hard enough you will find a note of hope.

Courage is not freedom from fear
but being frightened and going on.

**Have the courage
of your convictions.**

Don't dwell on dashed hopes.
Pick yourself up and start all
over again.

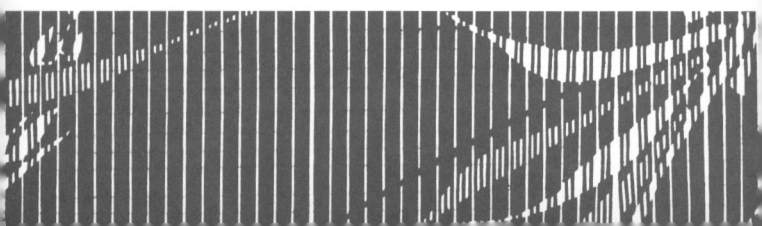

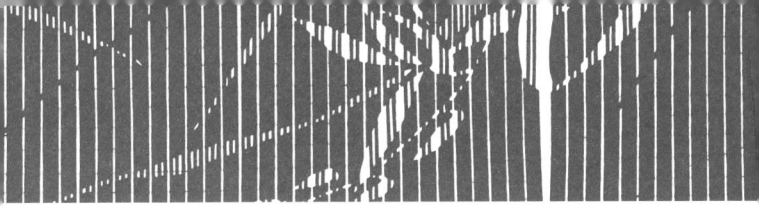

Deciding to change your thoughts from despair to hope has unbelievable power and will give you momentum.

See setbacks as learning curves rather than failures.

Life is too exciting to give up on. Step out with hope.

Rest your hopes in the future and try not to dwell on past disappointments.

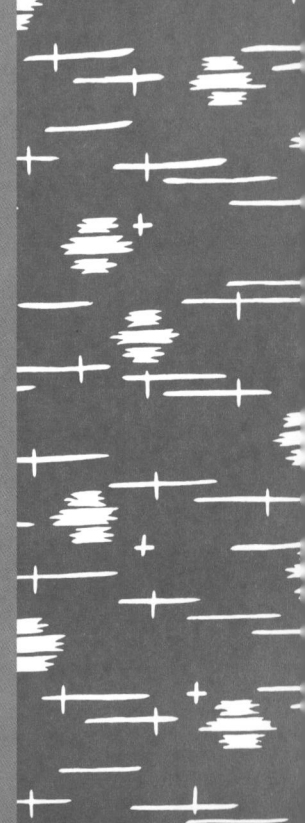

Try to pin your hopes on the big picture—don't get bogged down with small details.

Don't lose hope on account of a nasty comment or jibe. It's too easy to slip into a negative cycle of thinking.

Let harmful words pass over you. You are bigger than that. Draw strength from your inner hope.

If a bad thing happens, try to balance it with all the good things in your life so you don't lose hope.

The first step to building positive hope is to silence any negative inner whispers.

When you feel like giving up, hope is the tiny voice inside you saying, "Go on, give it a go—one more time."

No matter how difficult the situation, the only way to deal with it is with hope.

When everything around seems dark and hopeless, imagine all this is happening to someone else, and think of the hopeful words of encouragement you would give them. Then try saying them to yourself.

Hopeful affirmations can help build confidence and change negative behavioral patterns into positive ones. Start by replacing "it's not possible" with "perhaps."

If everything seems hopeless, think of it as a transitional phase rather than the milestone by which you will measure the future.

Remember tomorrow is another day.

There will be plenty more tomorrows.

Even after a bad harvest there must be a sowing.

Seneca

Hope is the other side of hopelessness. Which one would you choose?

If you have hope in your heart you are still alive.

It is never too late for hope.

There are no hopeless situations,
just people who think hopelessly.

You are the master of your thoughts. Choose to believe in your hopes.

If you believe things are hopeless the chances are you stop trying. As a result things can turn out just as you feared. Don't go there!

Your intentions create your reality, say the self-help gurus. So get hoping!

Human wisdom can be summed up in two words: wait and hope.
>Alexandre Dumas

If you have no hope, how can you ever achieve anything?

Someone once said that if you get in a car and don't know where you are going, you will never get there. Make sure you can identify your hopes.

Believe in yourself and your abilities—stop looking at others and look at your own qualities.

Being hopeful takes practice. It involves focusing on the positive aspects of your life.

When we meet real tragedy in life, we can react in two ways—either by losing hope and falling into self-destructive habits, or by using the challenge to find our inner strength.

If you have been knocked sideways, give yourself time to bounce back. But remember that sooner or later you must throw off the past and look forward with hope.

Look for something new to hope in if your dream turns out to be a real no-hoper.

Never presume that things will never change. Everything moves on.

Nothing can be done without hope and confidence.

Helen Keller

No one really cares if you are hopeless, so you might as well be hopeful.

Active thinking and physical activities can help to keep hope alive.

Keep your mind alert—read books, do crosswords, play sudoku, and go to movies. Join a book club or set up a weekly movie group.

Get moving—join the gym, go swimming, or take up a new sport.

If you don't have hope, how can you expect anyone else to hope in you?

Seeking help—whether through a friend or professional—can break the cycle of hopelessness.

Don't be frightened to share your hopes and fears.

Everything in your life can give you hope or make you despair; it's up to you to let it give you hope.

Hope depends on perseverance: the ability to keep going no matter what life throws at you.

The opposite of hope is giving up, abandoning ambition.

To live is to wrestle with despair, yet never to allow it to win over hope.

Despair is hope's worst enemy, so beware its evil hold.

Every moment of life is a new beginning as we move on from the old.

Hope is essential in every situation.

Without hope, the miseries of poverty, sickness, and war would be unbearable.

All of us are searching for hope—for the future, for peace, for happiness.

No matter how difficult our struggles, there is always hope.

See obstacles as stepping-stones to be negotiated.

"Dear God, give me hope!" is a common cry, but you will find hope a lot quicker if you start the ball rolling with some positive thinking.

All things are possible, and woe betides he who begs to differ.

Hopelessness is laying down the tools and giving up the fight. Don't go beyond the point of no return.

Hope is about choice: it is up to you whether you go forward with hope, stay still as you are, or look back with regret.

There are many sides to every story. Changing yours may bring hope where once there was only despair.

Seeing things in a different light can brighten the darkest moment.

Try to put a positive spin on negative thoughts.

Challenge irrational thoughts with rational positive thoughts and watch your self-talk become more hopeful.

The greatest misery is to be without a goal, to see no hopeful purpose in living.

Trapped and hopeless we cannot be happy.

To hope is to be free.

The pursuit of hope is part of life's rich tapestry, but it can be difficult to accomplish.

The trick to finding hope is to look in the right place.

Regret is only good for wallowing in. It is far better to step out of it with hope.

If you don't hope to win you have already lost.

Listening to the small voice in your heart can turn hope into a reality.

Remember life does not go backward, so don't dwell on yesterday.

See dashed hopes as a wake-up call, propelling you toward something bigger and better.

Hope goes hand in hand with happiness.

**Look on the bright side and you never know,
it may come to pass.**

Who says you can't do it?
You plant your own hopes.
Whether they bear fruit is
largely up to you.

Invest hope in yourself and watch how others start to put their hope in you.

Be your own hopeful friend.

Wish someone well every day.

If you're feeling low, heed this advice:
- Never read *Madame Bovary*
- Life's too short for Proust
- Don't even attempt Chekov's short stories

"I can't" is the enemy of hopeful thinking.

Instead of "I can't" try saying "I can."

Don't think you are the only one
to have your hopes dashed.
It can and does happen to us all.

**If something or someone does not
turn out as you hoped,
it does not mean there is something
wrong with you.**

If you don't achieve your hopes, don't
immediately assume you are a failure.
Maybe you need to approach things
from a different angle.

Think back to a past success: "If I did it then I can do it now."

See setbacks as challenges rather than failures waiting to happen.

Don't underestimate the power of humor. Laughter can give a spurt of hopeful energy.

Try to focus on the strategy as the problem rather than yourself.

As soon as you encounter a problem, look back to a similar situation and go over in your mind how you handled it that time.

When rekindling hope, some small but important changes in the way you think may be all that is required to kickstart it into action.

Always believe that you can change for the better and contribute to making the world a better place.

If you're feeling hopeless, tap into some positive memories and see hope begin to flower.

If you keep an elephant in your living room no one can get past it—including you. Confront your fears and watch them dwindle. Then see your hopes grow.

The capacity for hope is strengthened by adversity.

Hope that has never been challenged is a fragile web.

If you come across a sticky patch, take a step back and try to see the bigger picture of where your hopes lie.

Ask yourself what is the worst possible thing that could happen to you now. Is it really that hopeless?

You are bigger than any setbacks and you don't have to succumb to them.

Hope parries all blows.

To define someone as a hopeless case is to consign them to the scrapheap of humanity.

Hope for the best for your friends. It could be you one day.

A nation without hope is a nation without a future.

Don't worry about a thing. For every little thing gonna be all right.

Bob Marley

Hopelessness is a bad place to be.
Hopefulness is a good place to be.
To get out of the bad place, leave it
and go to the good place instead.

Thinking hopefully, no matter what happens, means you are far more likely to succeed in life because you don't give up so early. The longer you try, the more probable it is you are going to succeed.

Hopeful thinking helps people to see
the positives where others can't.

Hopeful thinking puts you on the lookout for the possibilities in new situations, rather than just the potential pitfalls.

When you instinctively start to see setbacks as temporary, and positive outcomes as inevitable, then you'll have picked up the hopeful habit.

When you think about it, what other choice is there but to hope?

We have two options, mentally and emotionally: give up, or fight like hell.

Don't lose hope in the future of the planet. You can make a difference:
- **Only fly when you have to**
- **Leave the car at home**
- **Recycle, recycle**
- **Switch off lights you are not using**

Enjoy the journey to your dreams.

Worrying will get you nowhere, and it certainly won't make you hopeful.

Do something about your worries rather than just obsessing about them: get a piece of paper and make a list of them. Nine times out of ten, seeing them on paper helps you view them in a different light.

What makes you lose hope? Try to identify the triggers so you can rationalize why you feel down when these situations arise.

When you are tired it's hard to feel hopeful about anything. Try to eat more of the following foods. All are rich in co-enzyme Q10—a naturally occurring substance that helps revitalize body and spirit.

- Tuna
- Spinach
- Sardines
- Sesame seeds
- Mackerel

Shakespeare described sleep as "the chief nourisher in life's feast," and what better way to boost mind, body, and spirit?

Feeling hopeless? Look at all the things that didn't go wrong today.

Experiencing lows is like putting on glasses—it helps you see things more clearly and appreciate the good things in life.

Get support. The hopeful journey should be fun, so ask a friend to join in.

Spend some time with a child—yours or someone else's. It can help to put things in perspective and put you back on the path to hope.

Remember you are resilient. The bigger the setback or challenge, the higher you will rise to meet it.

You have choices. Practice seeing choices everywhere and you'll soon be back in the hope zone.

Raise your hopes. Low hopes lead to low self-esteem.

Next time you find yourself in a hopeless situation, call it a challenge, not a problem. That way you are already thinking hopefully and will solve it more quickly.

If you wake up feeling low in hope don't despair. Just pull on your brightest-colored sweater. It's hard to feel down in the dumps when you're wearing fire-engine red or tangerine orange.

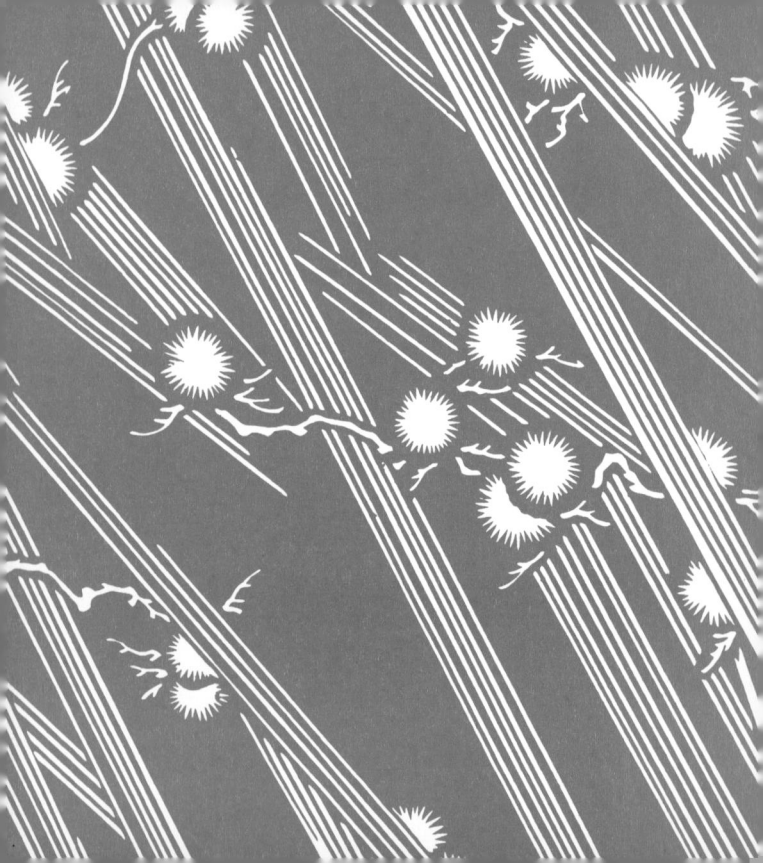

Hope
at Work

Hope is not a feeling of certainty that everything will be okay, but rather a feeling that life and work have meaning.

Make a wish list of the things you hope will happen at work, then put this plan into action.

No obstacle is insurmountable if you've got hope.

Follow your star.

Hope is the power that encourages you to go for that promotion.

Get colleagues to have hope in you—shrinking violets never win prizes.

It is better to try and fail than fail to try.

Hope is the engine of success. It is the spark that ignites our energy and drives us toward our career goals.

Let hope in and you immediately open the door to untold possibilities in the workplace.

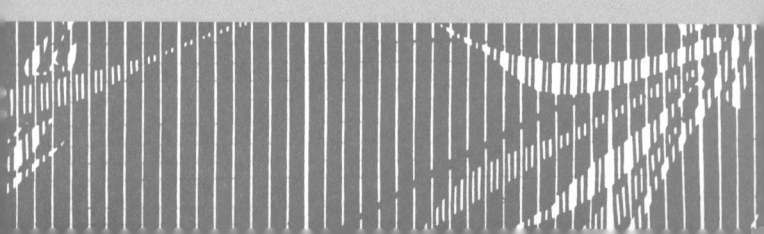

Keep on hoping and you increase your chances of success.

Limited hopes yield only limited results.

If you don't reach for the sky, you'll never know if you could get there.

If you don't make the choice to get what you want, who will?

Hope is realizing that what you want at work is possible, then working out how to get it.

Hopeful employees make for happy employees.

Hope is the chain that links one working day to the next.

You can dream forever, but only by doing something will you succeed.

Fulfilling your hopes could mean taking a risk. Be brave—fortune favors the brave.

Hope is when you sit up and decide to take action.

The stronger your hope, the more likely you are to act on it.

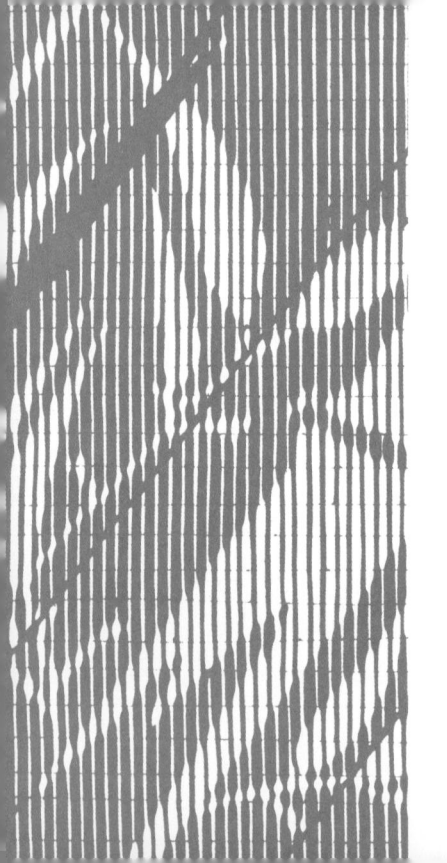

See the hope in every situation and you will succeed.

Once you decide to back hope all things are possible.

Hope means setting any goal you want to achieve and actually achieving it.

Clarifying your hopes will fill you with active and empowering thoughts.

Clearly defined goals enhance hope-related thinking and result in more positive outcomes.

When you love your work, you begin to develop all sorts of new hopes.

Discover what really drives you from within, then match it with real-life activities to give your life new hope and meaning.

Plan ahead, clarify your priorities, and stay focused.

Hope prepares you for whatever your boss throws at you.

Writing down your hopes can help you focus on them.

Hope is powerful—it helps the head and heart work together and encourages us to stretch ourselves mentally.

Hope keeps you on your toes. Make sure you've got plenty of it.

Hope will get you through the worst adversity at work.

Don't limit your hopes—hope for the limits.

No matter how satisfied you are with your job it does no harm to be on the lookout for something bigger and better.

Hope for more and you will experience more.

Don't give the same importance to all work goals. Prioritize the ones you hope to achieve first.

Hopes should not be so far beyond the realms of possibility that you are never likely to achieve them; on the other hand hopes should not be so easy that you are bound to achieve them.

Picture what you want, explore possibilities, and then be specific.

It's only by understanding your objectives that you can work out the relevant strategy to achieve them.

Make sure your hopes chime with the values of the organization you work for, and if they don't, it may be time to think about a change.

Hope is what moves you from where you are to where you want to be.

Hopes can take time to come to fruition. Remember much of the goodness of life comes from experiencing the journey, not simply arriving.

Identify your own big hopes and you're on your way to a happier working life.

The next step is to set up realistic steps to achieving your hopes.

Of all the things that make for a better work environment none is so powerful as hope.

Follow your hopes; trust your instincts.

Hope provides us with a destination and the motivation to get started.

Hope is the spring in your step as you go about your working day.

If you work hard and involve yourself, you will soon start to feel the sense of hope that comes from knowing that you are working to make things better.

Hope is important—it allows you to fly.

Big projects start from the smallest grain of hope.

Don't settle for less than you want.

Set your goals high
and fight for them.

**Nothing ventured,
nothing gained.**

Don't be put off by others' harsh words. They could be signs of insecurities or even envy.

**Have the courage
of your convictions.**

He who dares wins.

Hope is the process of linking
yourself to potential success.

You are never too old to succeed. Remind yourself that many people do not achieve their hopes until well into old age.

Visualize yourself fulfilling your hopes and reaching your goals, and enjoy the pleasure that this brings.

Keep your hope list simple and it will be more effective.

If your work is close to what you hope to be, you are more likely to enjoy it.

The hope of doing something that inspires you can keep you going.

Hope can make all the difference between dread and excitement when the alarm goes off in the morning.

If you fulfill your ambitions, you can be an inspiration and give hope to others.

Are you really doing what you want? Is your job satisfying? Are you fulfilling your potential? If what you are doing is going against your inner values, think how you could start changing things for the better.

A sure way to make hopes come true is to start living them now.

Get out of that rut. Expand your hopes and you will discover new vitality and confidence.

Do you believe that you deserve to fulfill your hopes? Make sure you do and you will increase your chances of them happening.

Replace "should" with "could" and watch your life's ambitions come true.

Hopes can be small as well as big.

Sometimes smaller hopes are easier to focus on initially, egging you on toward bigger ones in the future.

Don't dwell on what might have been.
Instead get on with making your next
hope come true. You never know,
it might even turn out better than
the hope you left behind.

Treat changes to plans as challenges to face up to rather than threats to your personal hopes.

Be flexible. You may have to reevaluate your hopes from time to time.

Remain true to your hopes. Whether you are making little or big plans it is important to remain true to yourself.

If your hopes are dashed, work out what you have gained from the experience and then move on.

Keeping a daily work diary can help put things in perspective.

Think about how you will do things next time.

See setbacks as a source of feedback, about what doesn't work and what could work, to help your hopes come true.

If things go wrong, apply what you have learned and change your tactics if necessary. Keep focusing on your hopes.

When you get a different outcome to the one you expected, let the unexpected guide you to a new and perhaps better future.

To hope is to recognize that every challenge is also an opportunity.

If you feel disheartened when things seem hopeless, try asking yourself questions such as, "What do I really want from this?", rather than "Why did this happen to me?"

Focus your energy on making the most of the situation, however hopeless it may seem.

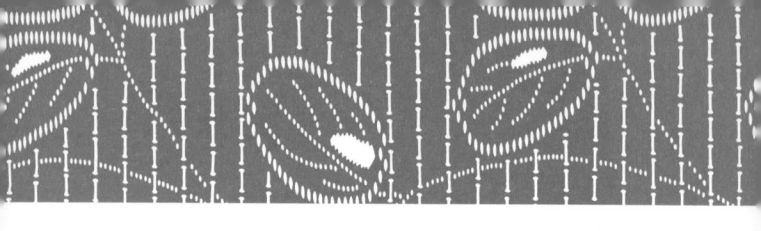

If you start to lose hope of achieving what you hope for, it can help to take a break to reevaluate and get things in perspective.

To move through setbacks, try behaving as if you have already achieved what you are hoping for. You'll be amazed how this builds up self-confidence and how obstacles start to diminish.

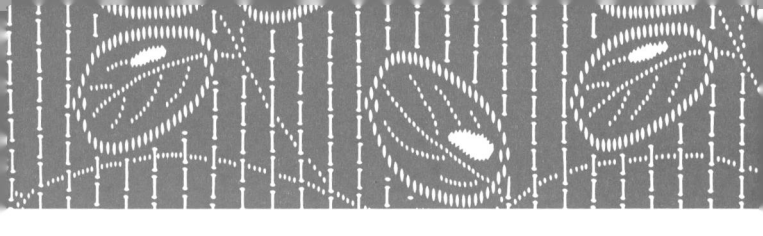

Recognize and reward your achievements. Seeing how much you have moved on keeps hope alive, giving you the confidence to go further.

You can gain hope just by the process of trying something.

Don't be swayed by others—you can be firm about your hopes if you work out in advance why you are doing something.

If you lose your job, for example by being laid off, use it as an opportunity to hope for a new and better life.

When one door closes another one opens.

Avoid complaining about being unemployed. Instead speak hopefully and positively. People respond to positive people.

When looking for a job, speak positively about your hopes and capabilities to prospective employers.

Talk about opportunities, and look for new ideas and new avenues to follow.

Looking at things differently can bring new hopes to your circumstances.

Hope makes the impossible possible.

Hopeful thoughts bring hopeful thinking, while bad thoughts bring bad thinking.

Discovering new skills can give you new hopes.

Changing your routine can help refresh your life, bringing new hopes.

Each dip is followed by a higher rise, and the overall pattern is upward and onward, making true the Latin motto *per ardua ad astra* (through endeavor to the stars).

A. C. Grayling

Think of daily problems as career challenges that arouse you.

Enjoy working to reach your hope and don't focus solely on the end goal.

Hopeful thinking enables you to find alternative ways to reach your goals if you find yourself stuck.

Physical exercise gives you physical energy, which in turn can infuse you with mental energy and hope.

Spending all day hunched over your computer can be the killer of hope. Take regular screen breaks and have a good stretch.

Shy away from setting hopes that other people think you should have.

Make sure your career choices are your own and stick to them.

Go over in your head different ways of fulfilling your hopes, and then choose and stick with the best route.

If you need a new skill to fulfill your hope make sure you acquire it sooner rather than later.

Installing the latest computer software is all very well but not knowing how to operate it is guaranteed to make you feel hopeless.

If you keep on doing what you've always done, you'll keep on getting what you've always got.

Stuck in a rut? Research shows that people who consciously start to change their thought patterns report an immediate improvement in their performance. Their energy increases, as do their hopes.

The most important things in the world have been accomplished by people who kept on trying when there seemed to be no hope at all.

If at first you don't succeed try, try again.

FIND HOPE IN:
- An annual bonus
- A word of praise from your colleagues
- A big thank you for hard work done
- A successful appraisal

Focus on what is working. If you focus on what isn't working you'll get more of the same.

Bosses and employees must have the same vision about the long- and the short-term goals of the business for a successful relationship.

For continued success, bosses and employees must regularly review their goals and look at how they are going to achieve them.

Bored stiff or stuck in a rut? Give that recruitment agency a ring. Yours could be the résumé they are waiting for.

People who are treated as though they are going to succeed are more likely to do so.

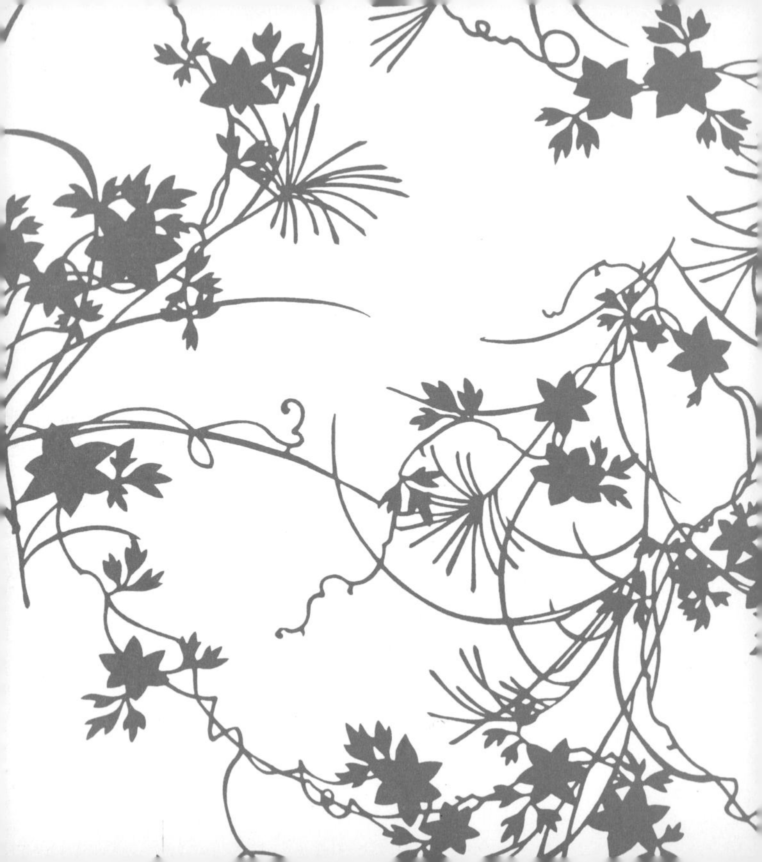

How can a person feel hopeful if they never receive praise for good work?

Don't settle for the ordinary. Strive for the extraordinary.

Having a hopeless day? Clearing your desk and tidying your files can give you the energy to follow your dreams.

Hope is catching. Instill some in colleagues and see how fast it spreads.

Do you really want to find yourself sitting in an armchair in your dotage saying to yourself:
"If only I had"?

Hope without an object cannot live.

Hope is based on the premise of getting from A to B.

If you achieve your small hopes, you're well on your way to achieving your big ones too.

Planning means you know where you are going and that everything you do is focused on achieving your hopes.

Make sure your home and workplace are as full of hopeful light as possible. If either is on the dark side, it may be worth investing in daylight simulation bulbs.

Hope is getting that interview for the perfect job.

Patience is a hopeful virtue.

Be aware of doors opening and walk through them.

Work hard,
hope hard,
play hard.

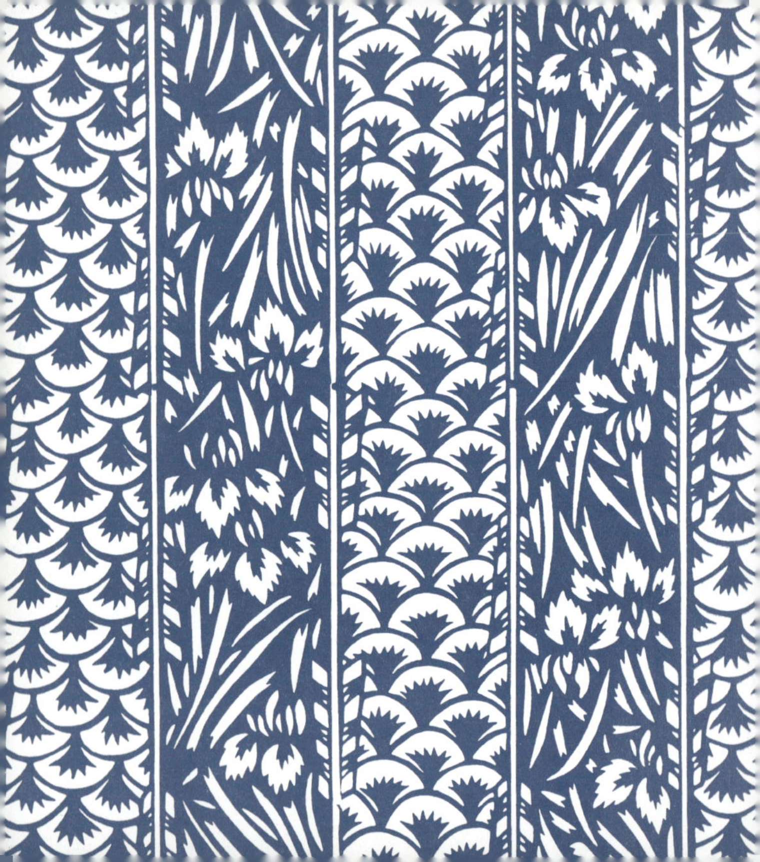

Hope and Relationships

Hope is the most exciting thing in life, and if you believe that love is out there it will come.

It is the hope of loving and being loved that keeps us going.

Hope nurtures love; love dies when hope is dead.

Put hope into someone else's life with a smile.

Love comes to those who still hope even though they have been disappointed.

Share your hopes and someone may help you to fulfill them.

To hope for love is to risk pain, but you must take risks in love because the greatest sadness in life is to love nothing or no one.

At the beginning of any love affair we are consumed with hope. Don't let it die.

New love can resurrect hope.

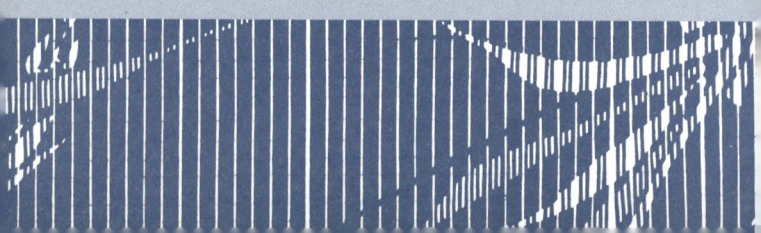

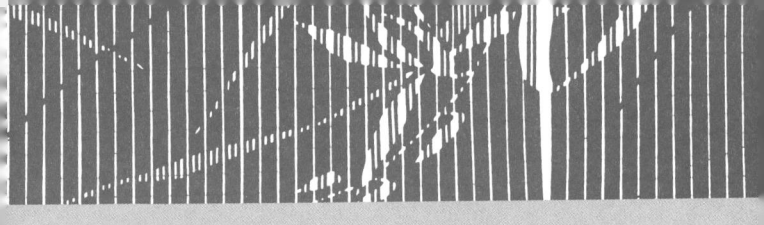

When you decide not to see someone again remember you are a moment in their story, so make it a story that fills them with hope for their future happiness.

Hope is giving your friend a hug.

Hope breeds hope—surround yourself with hopeful people.

The richest relationships are based on shared hopes.

People who build hope in their lives and share hope with others become powerful.

Talk continually to each other about how you feel, your hopes, and your dreams.

Sharing emotions can strengthen the hopeful bond between people.

Use friends as sounding-boards. Talking through your hopes can help clarify your thoughts.

If a partner or friend expresses an unrealistic hope don't ridicule it. Enter into the spirit of the hope ("I can see how that could make you happy") and let them work out whether it is achievable or not.

Find out what you really want by looking at what you envy in others. Your envious feelings can be used to unearth your secret hopes.

Hope and the world hopes with you.

Remember to show your support and appreciation for the people who place their hope in you. These are the most important people in your life.

When you start to show hope
in someone else you will start
to feel hopeful yourself.

Don't forget other people in your rush to achieve your hopes.

Don't dwell on what might have been in relationships. Use the information to make your future hopes bigger and brighter.

Avoid situations where others squash inspiration and hope with negativity or, worse still, put-downs.

The frame of mind you are in can dictate how you deal with people today and every day. Make it hopeful.

Positive thinking means keeping an open, hopeful mind when meeting someone for the first time.

Being hopeful makes life much more pleasant, not just for you but also for everyone you meet.

Remember, we all stumble, every one of us. That's why it's a comfort to go hand in hand.

When you radiate hope and vitality and truly care for others, you send out a strong invitation for love.

One of the most important prerequisites for finding a loving relationship is believing that you will.

Your relationship can be a beacon of hope to the outside world as you show devotion, love, humor and understanding to each other.

You discover more about people when you learn about their hopes than when you count their achievements, for the best of what we are lies in what we hope to be.

A. C. Grayling

Never deprive someone of hope: it may be all they have.

Hopeful people have give-and-take relationships in which both parties gain from the interchange.

Friendship is an opportunity for new hope.

Hopes are planted in friendship's garden where dreams blossom into priceless treasures.

Anon

You can't choose your family
but you can choose your friends.

**Surround yourself with
people who support you
in your dreams.**

Friends comfort and stroke each other with hopeful words. Make sure you have a good circle of them.

An important part of friendship is sharing hopes and tips on how to reach them.

Make sure your friendships are two-way, so you are receiving hope as well as giving it.

There is no friend like a sister to lift one up in hopeless moments.

If you are not establishing warm relationships with people chances are you are not hopeful about yourself as a friend.

To build up friendships in your life you may have to go out and find them. Try to put yourself in situations where interactions are likely to occur.

Friendships help bolster hopeful thinking.

One of the greatest rewards is to see the hopes of those you care about fulfilled.

Hopeful people bring inspiration and life to their interactions with all those around them.

Hopeful thinking influences our
relationships with others, and
our relationships with others
have an impact on our hope.

**When a relationship gets into
trouble it is usually because the
two partners do not share the
same hope, i.e. moving things on
to marriage or living together.**

We need to look at each other every
day with clear eyes and an open mind,
so we see the person of today,
not an image from the past.

There can only be hope for society if we work together, not separately.

Marriage is a single hope living within two bodies.

Hopefulness can work its magic on others as well as yourself.

Hope is the bond that binds two people together.

Hope flourishes when love abounds. Make room for plenty of love in your life.

Shared hopes make relationships steadfast and strong.

A twinkle in an eye across the room means that hope is alive and kicking.

Never write someone off as hopeless. Giving them a chance may bring back hope into their life.

Sharing hopes as a family will help to keep you together forever.

Think how good you feel when someone places their hope in you. Now, why not try it on someone yourself?

Talk about your hopes with your friends and ask them to support you as you set out on your journey.

Yours might not always be the best route to getting what you hope for. Listen to what others have to say and a new perspective may emerge.

No man is an island: we are all dependent on each other.

If you give support you are more likely to receive it, so don't hold back on the giving.

There must be plenty of give and take in any hopeful exchange.

Hopeful people bring a liveliness and vigor to their interactions with others.

Hope plays a vital part in all our important relationships.

Mutual hope, for example between doctor and patient, may help accelerate healing.

Relationships where those involved make it possible for the other to achieve their hopes produce a caring yet active environment where things get done.

A successful relationship depends on both parties setting reachable targets, and then giving each other enough space to go about achieving them.

Put your hope in someone else and you could be doing them an enormous favor.

How can you expect someone to believe in you if you don't believe in yourself?

People who are interested in life and full of hope are more interesting and more attractive to others.

We all hope we will meet the person of our dreams but it doesn't always just happen. Sometimes you have to start the ball rolling.

Answering that lonely-hearts ad could be the first step toward a hopeful, happy, long-term partnership.

Instill hope in family and in friends by acknowledging those special moments with a card, for example:
- **Passing exams**
- **Engagements**
- **New job**
- **Retirement**
- **New baby**

According to Zen Buddhism, if you conjure up an image of the person you want to meet, describe them very carefully, set your intent and "send it to the Universe," you will attract the one you are looking for.

In any ongoing relationships you need to cocreate hopes.

As your relationship grows your hopes may need to change. Be aware of your partner's needs and react accordingly.

Telling your friends and family about your hopes can help to spur you into action.

Encouragement can be hope's best fuel.

Our children are our hopes for tomorrow.

You are the bows from which your children are sent forward as arrows; you can help to make it a hopeful journey.

C. R. Snyder

Children who experience hope are more likely to pass it on to their children.

Children hunger for hope and respond to an environment that allows and nurtures it.

Teach children to choose the right path, and when they are older, you increase the chances of them staying on it.

It is a parent's job to pass on hope and keep it alive in their children.

Children flourish in a home with a hopeful atmosphere.

Children have a natural enthusiasm for goals and it is a parent's duty to cultivate their determination to pursue them.

Watch children from an early age, notice where their focus is, and help them explore and map out goals in their small worlds.

Children should put their hopes into words as much as possible.

Encourage children to talk about the pros and cons of each hope and to compare the alternatives.

Stumbling blocks are essential childhood experiences that train them to think hopefully.

Praise children whenever they show determination to fulfill their hopes.

You may not agree with the direction of your children's hopes but it is their life and what right have you to dictate it?

Tell children that hopes going wrong should be seen as challenges rather than preludes to failure.

Remember your children's hopes should be theirs, not yours or their sister's or brother's.

If your child seems to be floundering in one area don't lose hope. Instead focus on another area where they are successful and build on it.

Listen carefully to children so you can help them identify their real hopes.

If children have conflicting hopes, show them how this could be a problem and show them ways to resolve the conflict.

Children will become more hopeful if you praise their achievements.

Try not to push children to hope for the impossible.

Nobody can make you feel hopeless without your consent.

Strong relationships can help propel you toward fulfilling your vision and the life you hope for.

What you give out tends to be reflected back to you by those around you. For example, if you are feeling hopeful about people, they are more likely to feel hopeful toward you.

Tapping into the powers of others can lift your hopes.

Treat people with respect and respond to their hopes.

Surround yourself with people who can help you take your hopes to the next stage.

We attract the people we hope for.

All relationships are reflections of the one you have with yourself, so make sure yours is hopeful.

We feel at our most positive and optimistic about life when we are communicating and working successfully with others.

Give someone a hug. Touching and being touched can restore hope in life and love.

Making love can fill you with hope and this is why: As the brain revs up for sex, the production of stress hormones such as cortisol drops dramatically. The result is a long, glorious, hopeful high!

Hope is a roomful of strangers.

Hope is like trust, and the stronger it is, the stronger your love will be.

To tread on someone's hope is to tread on their dreams.

Don't keep hope to yourself— shout about it for all to hear.

Living
Hopefully

Hope is what makes living bearable.

You create your life in this moment, so you can commit yourself to hope right now.

Hope keeps life alive.

He who hopes wins.

Hope is yours for the taking.

Hope nurtures our dreams—both waking and sleeping.

Tune in to hope and you tune in to life.

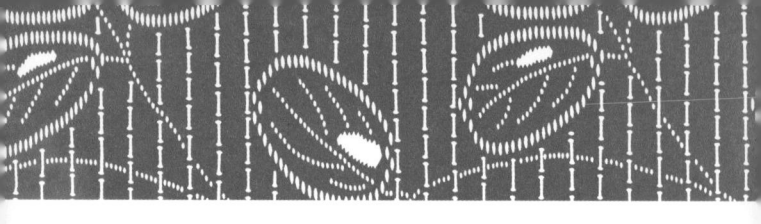

Hope for the best but be ready for the worst.

Breathe hope in every breath you take.

Hope is addictive—make sure you get hooked.

Hope may be directed
toward something minor
or toward something
extremely significant.

**Be hopeful and watch your
spirits soar.**

Hope is the sky
at the end of the tunnel.

Live life without fear; confront all obstacles and believe you can overcome them with hope.

Homing in on hope is homing in on happiness.

Hope is the precursor of happiness.

Hope can help you change the way you think and optimize your chances of happiness.

Happiness lies in setting yourself targets and putting your all into reaching them.

Plant a seed of hope and reap a bunch of happiness.

Do you have regrets about things you have never tried? Try them now. Don't leave any possibility for regret in your life.

**Don't wait too long before putting your hopes into action,
or it may be too late.**

A hopeful heart
is a happy heart.

When your heart is filled with hope, others will want to reach out to it.

Hope makes the world go round.

Use your energy to look to a positive future, a future full of hope.

**Dreams can come true
if you believe in them.**

Enjoy building the
hopeful life you were
meant to live.

**If you don't have hopes
they can never come true.**

You can have everything you want if you want it desperately enough.

A glimmer of hope and faith
will help you to see your way forward.

Fear can keep us up all night long, but hope makes one fine pillow.

Each day is full of opportunities.
If you do not recognize them,
it will carry them silently away.

Dum spiro, spero.
(While I breathe, I hope.)
　　　　　Latin proverb

Satisfaction is about how you evaluate your life and what you hope for in the long-term.

Take control of your hopes. Set big hopes then break them down into smaller daily aims. As you achieve each one you will feel more in control of your destiny.

Although life may not turn out exactly how you hoped, while you are here you must enjoy it.

Life is about hopes and dreams. Forget about what you have tried and failed at and focus on what you can still achieve.

Remember that you are not responsible for the misfortunes in your life, but you are responsible for doing something about them.

Bad times will pass. Everything changes and hope will return.

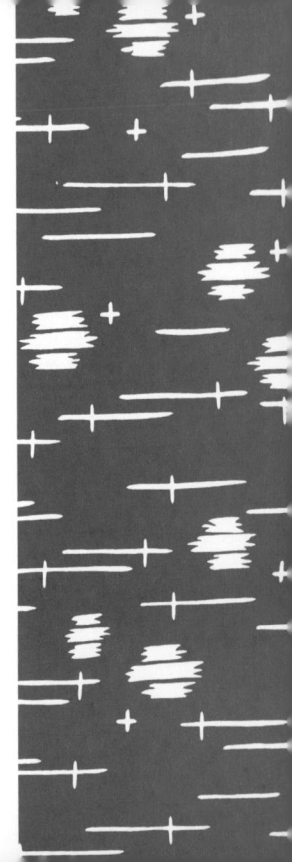

**If you don't believe in
fulfilling your hopes
they will never be fulfilled.**

Look for the hope in your life and your
life will become a hopeful experience.

You are never too old
to live hopefully.

Keep looking and listening—making learning a way of life will help you achieve your greatest hopes.

The old you is only the new hopeful you waiting to be undressed.

Get the most out of life
by becoming very hopeful.

Remember you are the most important person you will ever meet, so make sure you are full of hope and happiness.

Make positive, hopeful affirmations about yourself, and your life will become a hopeful experience.

Change is like a breath of fresh air. Enjoy the new hopes it brings.

Hope is your best bedfellow.

Hope is staring you in the face. Don't ignore it.

Humanity is full of hope. See it in your neighbors who look after you when you have lost your key, the knock of the mailman delivering that long-awaited package, or the window cleaner who makes your house gleam.

The only way to realize your hopes is to go for them.

Life would be very dull without a few hopes to pep it up.

Do things differently and watch new hopes emerge.

Enjoy the process of making things happen and enjoy the present. Remind yourself of these positive thoughts to help you focus on your hopes.

Program your brain into feeling hopeful. Get into the habit of thinking about the future in terms of all the good things it can bring.

Any experience, good or bad, can help build up hope for the future, if you are open to the message.

Make your hopes big and take chances in life. Unless you do, you will never know if they were meant to be.

Being inspired by something or someone is a great way to build up hope. It is also very empowering and confidence-building.

You can hope for anything you want to—how empowering is that?

Don't indulge your fears. Spend the time looking at your hopes and dreams.

Let hope be the light in your life. And remember the brighter it is, the brighter your world will be.

Make hope your signpost and you will never lose your way.

Hope and the world hopes with you.

If you have built castles in the air, your work need not be lost; that is where they should be. Now put the foundations under them.

Henry Thoreau

**Every house begins
with a brick of hope.**

A hopeful home is one where we protect, love, and care for younger family members to provide continuity and hope.

Make sure your house is a haven of hope.

Use mirrors to reflect hopeful views into your home.

Hang wind chimes by your front door—their chime will uplift your spirits as you enter.

Groups of snapshots of your kids placed in strategic places can help keep hope alive.

A garden can be a place for meditation, contemplation, and relaxation. Fill it with inspiring flowers—roses, freesias, lilies.

The Star of Bethlehem is the flower of hope.

Plant daffodils and hyacinths in fall and plant hope for a flower-filled spring.

Invest some hope in your future by investing in a:
- **personal trainer**
- **financial advisor**
- **nutritionist**

Hope doesn't stand still: make sure you run with it.

Hope is a shooting star in a dark night. We can choose to notice or ignore it, unaware that our destiny may hang in the balance.

Each new generation brings new hope.

Study self-help books to inspire you.

Hope is better than want because it injects passion, and passion is a strong motivator.

Hope is the passport to positive thinking.

Find hope in music and listen to:
- **Dusty Springfield's *Wishing and Hoping*...**
- ***All You Need is Love* by The Beatles**
- ***Dancing in the Dark* by Bruce Springsteen**

Hope can help you to break free from the burdens of life—to start replacing trials with tribulations.

**Hope costs nothing—
it is yours for the taking.**

Bank on hope and watch the interest accrue.

Without hope even the most agreeable pursuits become tedious.

The pursuit of hope is a lifelong affair.

Doing what is difficult can help restore hope, even though it may not seem so as you do it.

What we experience is what we construct, so living hopefully must be worked at.

Life without hope is like the sky without the sun.

Life can be strengthened by hope. To hope can be one of the greatest pleasures of living.

Never give up on your hopes and dreams; the path may be twisted and rocky but the world is waiting for your contribution.

You have to live by your own rules and discover your hopes for yourself.
Don't try to copy others.

If you don't fill life with hope it fills with fear instead.

Hope can be just a glimmer.
It's up to you to keep it alight.

By repeating an affirmation over and over again, it becomes embedded in your subconscious mind, and eventually becomes your reality.

**Hopes are like dominoes:
they build on each other.**

It takes hope to dare to do something,
but nine times out of ten the rewards
will far outweigh the fear.

**Prioritize your hopes
over your wants.**

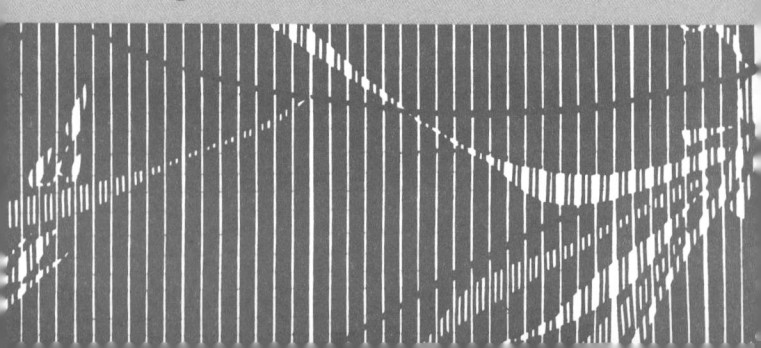

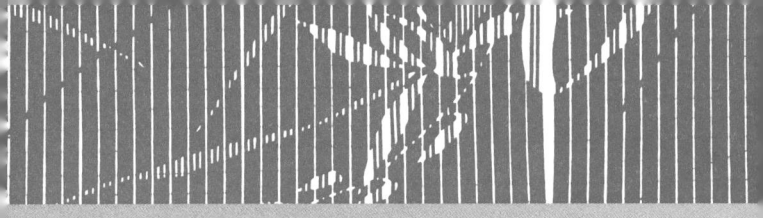

Hope is about saying you have learned from the experience.

You can and you will fulfill your hopes. It's all a matter of getting the route right.

All roads lead to hope, but expect to turn a few corners before you get there.

Working out the why and the wherefore can make the impossible seem possible.

Make sure that your ambitions are what you really want rather than what your mother or father or your partner hoped for you.

Avoid setting hopes according to the perceived standards of others.

If you want to bring change into your life, it is sometimes necessary to turn off your automatic pilot and to start thinking consciously about the small things that you do without thinking.

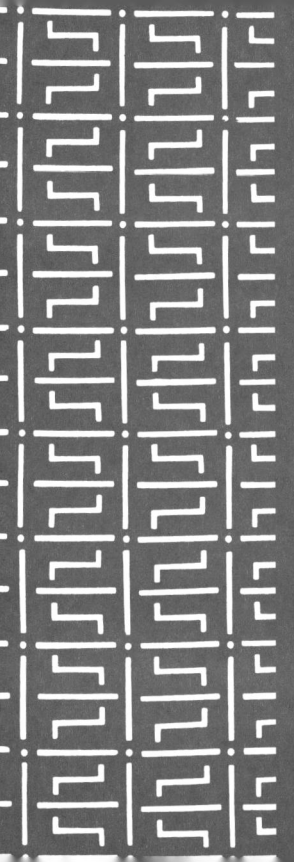

Open up your thinking by imagining hopes that seem far fetched, then ask yourself why not? It can be very liberating.

When thinking about your hopes take it slowly. Rushing can decrease your ability to choose the right ones for you.

Make sure your hope doesn't depend on other people changing—you can never guarantee a change in other people. The only person you can have that kind of control over is yourself.

Make a list of five things that give you most hope and do them on a regular basis.

A sense of humor can help protect you when all seems hopeless.

When things seem hopeless:
- Call a friend
- Bake a cake
- Tidy your cupboards
- Read a poem

Long-term hopes are like magnets that draw you in one direction while you focus on the ongoing journey.

A well thought-out hope produces ideas—how to achieve them will automatically follow.

When you have achieved one goal, next time set your hopes a little higher.

You may need to springclean your life, clearing the decks so you gain more energy, space, and clarity to help you achieve your hopes.

Use the past and present to help you shape your future hopes.

Hope, believe, achieve.
All things are possible.

Make hope your daily mantra.

Boost your energy and surround yourself with hopeful people.

Start getting rid of "if onlys" and start turning hopes into realities.

The link between what was and what might be rests in our hopes of today.

To nurture hope, live for today and let tomorrow take care of itself.

Experience today as if it is your first bowl of ice cream.

The more hopeful you feel on the inside, the more this will be reflected on the outside and in your immediate environment.

You can be all you hope to be.

You have the power to change your own reality.

Believe in your hopes and know you deserve the best things in life.

Speak up and express your hopes. You will never get what you want unless you ask for it.

You can change any self-beliefs that aren't working for you.

Comfort zones are only comfortable until we outgrow them.

Try something different:
- Take a salsa class
- Sign up for a language course
- Learn to play bridge

Think of a series of hopeful statements and try saying them aloud before bed. Hopefully they will enter your subconscious mind, which will assimilate them as reality while you sleep.

Remember you are likely to go through a series of ups and downs on your path to hope.

Drowning hopelessness in drink never did anyone any good. It may give a quick burst of hope but it won't last.

Avoid quick-fix stimulants such as coffee, alcohol, and nicotine.

Boost hopeful moods with natural fruit juices and invigorating herbal teas like ginger and peppermint.

Try herbal hope-boosters:
- **guarana**
- **ginseng**
- **St. John's wort**

Avoid moods that swing between hope and despair by following a mood-enhancing diet. This means including plenty of fruit and vegetables, wholefoods, seeds, and wheatgerm.

Chocolate is not all bad. It's full of serotonin-boosting sugar, mind-soothing fat, and other chemicals that favorably affect brain messengers controlling mood, say the experts. Just don't overdo it!

Vitamin D is not called the "the hormone of sunlight" for nothing; it is said to boost levels of serotonin —a feel-good chemical—in the brain.

Stroking a dog or simply watching an aquarium fish can fill the heart with hope.

Caring for a pet can help fend off hopelessness by bringing back responsibility and meaning to life.

A gentle massage can activate the receptors in skin that release endorphins, the body's own feel-good hormones.

Dance your way to hope—try flamenco, jive, or belly dancing.

Think about your ideal life—where you would like to be in two, five, or even ten years. Do your hopes bring you closer to that picture? If so, stick with them.

Change your hopes if you must but stay focused on the end point.

Stretch your way to hope. It gets the oxygen circulating around your body, filling you with energy.

Research shows that hope and optimism can help reduce your risk of cardiovascular diseases, diabetes, respiratory tract infections, high blood pressure, and colds.

Let hope change your life and take you forward to a better future.

According to ancient Chinese wisdom, clutter represents blocked energy and can bring your spirits down. Have a good clear out and look forward to a brighter, more hopeful future.

Surrounding yourself with beautiful objects that you love is a powerful way of creating hope in your home. Every time they catch your eye, you'll get a positive rush of hope.

Open fires, with the crackle and smell of burning wood and coals, can inspire great hope.

Smile—the very action of lifting the corners of your mouth into a smile floods your brain with serotonin.

Get out in the sunshine. Sunlight is a natural booster.

Have some fun—taking life a little less seriously can be incredibly uplifting. Pretend you are a child for a moment—start a water fight, throw pillows at your partner, splash around in some puddles, or try catching leaves in the park.

Think how good you feel when someone offers to carry your groceries or offers you their seat on the train. Now do it for someone else and help nurture their hope.

Feeling down in the dumps? Eating an oat-based cereal bar naturally sweetened with honey and fruit can help to put you in a more hopeful mood.

Forget processed, refined foods. Instead choose home-cooked wholesome foods such as broiled fish, fresh fruit and vegetables. They are full of vitamins and minerals that can help protect against long-term lows.

Get your day off to a hopeful start with an uplifting wake-up shower. Alternating blasts of hot and cold water will kickstart your metabolism and boost your circulation, encouraging oxygen-rich blood to reach every tissue of your body.

Set aside a weekend for a spring clean. Dust away the cobwebs, polish the windows, tidy the cupboards, and look forward to a brighter, cleaner future.

Charity begins at home: be kind and instill hope in all around you.

Hope is buying a five-year diary.

A hopeful life is about commitment to learning, work, family, friends, and worthwhile causes.

Remember it is never too late to start hoping for something new.

It is possible to learn to be hopeful without changing a thing in your life except your relationship to your own thinking.

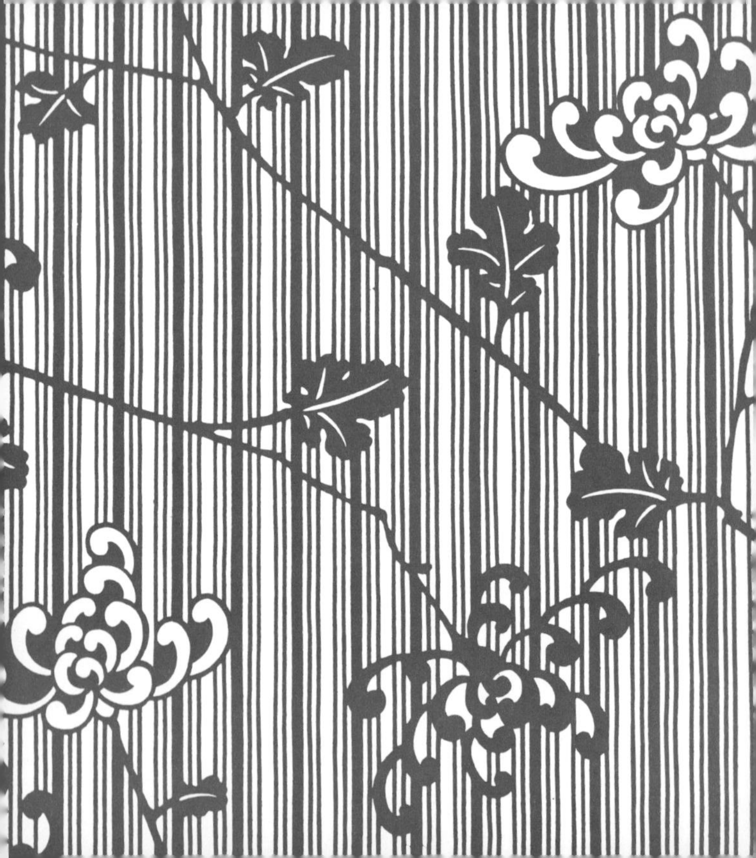

What is Hope?

Hope is life's must-have.

Hope is an attitude—
a way of approaching
the day's challenges.

Hope is change,
and change creates
opportunity.

**Hope is the answer
when all else fades away.**

Hope is what gives
our lives purpose.

**Hope is a candle that lights
the darkness of despair.**

The desire for happiness is in the center of all our hearts. It sustains us, frees us from discouragement, stops us being selfish, and leads to happiness.

Hope is grief's best music.

Anon

Hope happens when pessimism loses its hold.

Hope is the belief that even when things are not going well they will work out okay in the end.

Hope requires the long view.

Hope implies perseverance, believing that something is possible even when there is evidence to the contrary.

Hope is the dream of a soul awake.

French proverb

Hope is the last thing that dies in us.

Hope is the power that helps you step out and try.

Hope won't let you down.

Hope is not logical, so indulge your wildest dreams.

Hope is trying to see the good in everyone.

To hope means to be ready at all times for the unexpected.

Hope is seeing your glass half full rather than half empty.

Hope is the feeling that how you are feeling can and will change.

Hope is recognizing an opportunity as soon as it presents itself and going for it.

Hope is the star that shines the brightest in the night sky.

Hope is as big as life itself.

There is hope in the sun rising;
there is hope in the sun setting.

LOOK FOR HOPE IN:
- **The chatter of children on the school bus**
- **The smile or touch of a loved one**
- **The green shoots of spring or the falling leaves of autumn**

Hope is the breath
that inspires our lives.

**You begin your life with hope.
It's up to you to nurture it as
you journey through it.**

Hope is not the feeling that something will turn out right, but the belief that it is right, however it turns out.

People who express hope for others tend to be happier than those who are preoccupied with themselves.

Blind hope is when you're booked in for the plastic surgeon.

Hope is the thin thread of life when despair descends.

Hope is that crucial percentage of life.

Hope is a twinkle in the eye, the warmth in a handshake, or the comfort in a pat on the back.

Espero ergo sum.
(I hope therefore I am.)

Every time you speak out for what you believe you project hope.

Hope is putting faith to work when doubting would be easier.

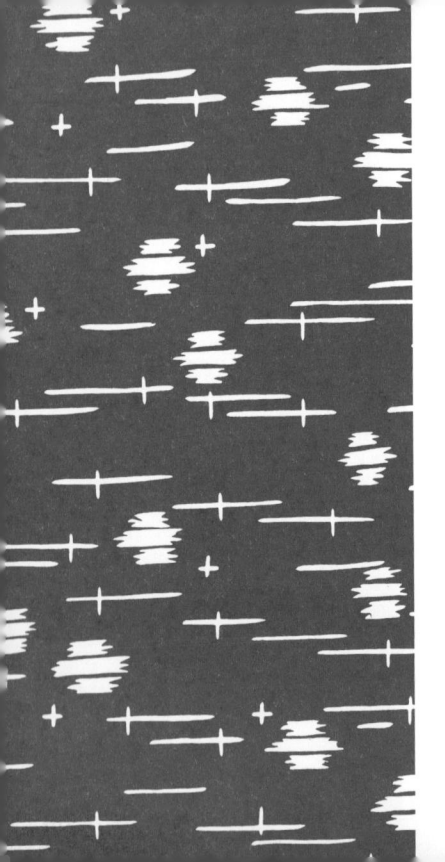

Hope is when you sit up and decide to take action.

Hope charges your spirit, giving you the strength to look forward to a better tomorrow.

Walk with hope in your heart and you will never walk alone.

Each new generation brings new hope.

To live in hope is to continue anticipating that something will happen.

A false hope is one based on fantasy or an unlikely outcome.

To hope is to long and to dream.

To hope against hope is to hope with little reason or justification, but still to believe that things will turn out all right.

To hope is to wish for something with expectation of its fulfillment.

To have hope is to have confidence and trust.

Hope is love's best friend.

Nurture hope and watch it grow.

Hope may be hiding but go on looking and you will find it.

Hope is on every horizon, however far away, so get out your telescope.

Hope is the enemy of despair and the friend of happiness.

The three ingredients for happiness are: something to do, someone to love, and something to hope for.

Hope is desire and expectation rolled into one.

Hope's door is open to all who want to enter.

Hope is a state of mind we can all experience.

Hope is a Saturday night dance.

Hope is waiting for exam results.

Hope is the dawn chorus.

Hope is knowing that people, like kites, are made to be lifted up.

                        Anon

Hope doesn't stand still.

Hope is always working for you.

Hope can lie in the throw of dice, the turn of a wheel or the number on a scratch card.

Hope builds on hope—it is the building block of life.

Hope deferred maketh the heart sick.

            Proverb

**Hope is a promise
of better things to come.**

**In bad times, hope is a
comfort that sustains the
idea of relief or rescue.**

Hope is a positive attitude full
of possibility and aspiration.

Hope is waiting for:
- The phone to ring when he said he'd call
- The check they said they'd mailed to arrive
- Your offer to be accepted on your dream house
- Your first novel to go into print

Hope is putting the baking powder into the cake mixture before it goes in the oven.

Hope is a four-letter word that can make things possible.

Hope is the smell of your mother's warm baked bread on a Sunday morning.

Hope is getting out in the court and playing a game of doubles in the middle of winter.

Hope is the foundation of all healing.

When you are unwell, hope is imagining an army of your white blood cells fighting off the invader.

Doctors turn research into hope for many thousands of their patients.

Hope is the hidden ingredient in any doctor's prescription.

**Dreams should be dreamt
and enthused about.
They can come true.**

Hope encourages us to move forward despite setbacks.

Hope advises us to look squarely at the realities that confront us while remaining aware of the possibilities.

Hope entails anticipating future happiness and trusting in the present to help us achieve it.

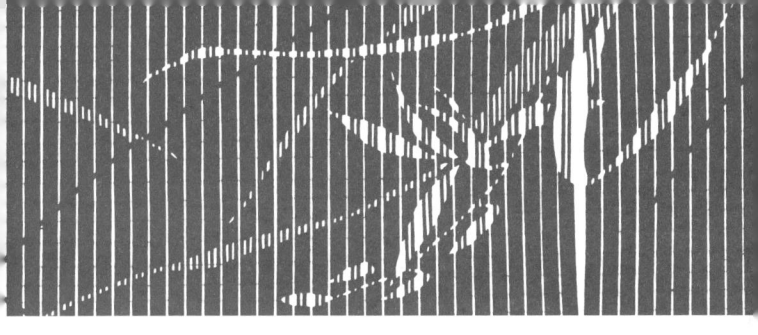

Hope is in love with success rather than failure.

All utopias are driven by hope.

Hope is seeing white where others see black.

Hope is watching dolphins playing in the sea.

Despair is the past tense, hope is the future perfect.

Hope is a never-ending stream.

Hope is the chime of the church clock.

Hope is the good of the world.

Hope is a newborn baby.

Hope is your grandchild's first smile.

Hope is the sister of optimism and the mother of achievement.

The girl's name Hope is of old English origin and means expectation.

Hope is:
- **The end of a rainbow**
- **Drying the clothes on a line in the fresh air**
- **A slow smile**

Hope likes to travel. You show it when:
- **Booking your summer vacation at Christmas**
- **Visiting a new continent**
- **Checking in your luggage at an airport**
- **Trusting the pilot at the controls**
- **Waiting at the carousel on arrival**

Hopelessness is the despair felt when all hope of comfort and success has been abandoned.

"Hopingly" means in a hopeful manner.

Hopeful is someone who aspires to success or shows promise of success, especially as a political candidate.

Hopefulness is the feeling you have when you have hope.

Just as hope begets hope so hopelessness begets hopelessness.

Hope rises above frustration and keeps us looking for something better.

The cycles of Nature are hope in action.

The determination of human beings is the world's biggest source of hope.

The ultimate tragedy in life is not death; it is the loss of hope.

Real hope is found in committing yourself to huge goals and dreams, such as a world without war and violence where everyone can live with dignity.

Hope is as essential to life as food and water.

Having hope in the future and ourselves is what enables us to go on in the face of disaster and conflict.

**Life without friendship
is a car without wheels.**

**Having faith is about
bringing forth the sun of
hope from your own heart
no matter what
circumstance you find
yourself in.**

The smallest things —like a robin perching at your bird table or the leaves turning red in fall – can hold great hope. Don't pass them by.

Hope is an invite arriving in the post.

Hope is Big Ben chiming in the New Year.

Hope is a break in the clouds.

Hope is rising above
the ozone layer.

Hope is the first page of a book.

Hope is the bite of a fish
at the end of the line.

Hope is writing a book that inspires others to hope.

Spiritual Hope

The three great virtues the New Testament calls for in Christians are faith, hope, and charity.

Trust your instincts. They will lead you to the true you.

Hope is the theological virtue defined as the desire and search for a future good, difficult but not impossible to attain with God's help.

In Christianity, faith has been described as the foundation of the building, love as the building itself, and hope as the windows of that building.

Faith goes up the stairs that love has built and looks out of the window that hope has opened.

Love is the greatest, hope is the least written about, and faith is necessary for salvation, but they can't be separated.

Love overcomes hate; hope overcomes despair; faith overcomes the face of evil.

Belief in God and trusting his promises can fill lives with hope.

Hope is the basis of all religion. If you believe, you hope.

The Bible is a source of hope and help for all who place their faith in God. Try reading it.

Spirituality is easily identified in people who have hope and trust in God's mercy, wisdom, and justice.

Hope is kneeling down beside your bed and saying your night prayers.

Let hope inspire your prayers.

All things bright and beautiful,
the lord God made them all.

Looking at something beautiful in nature, objects, or people shows your capacity to love. This immediately opens up your heart and allows loving energy inside.

Angels are bearers of hope.

Reach for the moon even though you have got the stars.

In Christianity the ultimate hope is for life after death. Some call it heaven.

Hope is the key to heaven's door.

Heaven is not a place but a state of mind you can create every day of your life with hope.

Hope is the promise of life eternal.

Cherish your ability to believe and hope.

Hymns are songs of hope and praise.

He who
hopes has
no fear.

Hope is as essential to a good death as it is to a good life.

Hope and happiness are true bedfellows.

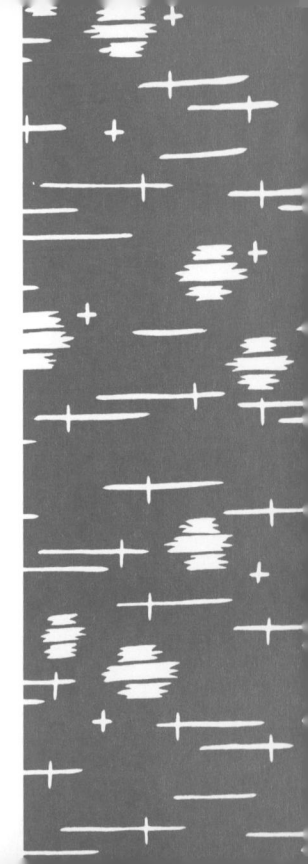

Make space in your life both physically and emotionally, and you will feel hopeful and in control.

Look into the past to find the clues you need to change your future, then let go of the past.

Slow down your breathing, your talking, your pace. Take time to nurture your inner hope.

When you can see hope in your mind's eye you draw it into your real experience.

Your sense of the spiritual does not depend on spiritual beliefs. Your spirituality lies within you.

Follow things through, let your hopes become your reality.

**The only inner strength that matters is the kind that gets you from one moment to the next.
You can call it hope.**

There are two sides to every day. You can approach it from the side of anxiety or the side of hope and faith.

Do not be afraid of tomorrow, for hope is already there.

Life without room for hope is too narrow a space in which to live.

According to Dante, at the entrance of hell is the following sign:
"Leave every hope you who enter."

Hope transcends death.

Hope is your guardian angel. Show her respect and she will look after you.

Miracles are hope in action. If you don't believe in them they will never happen.

According to Buddhist doctrine, we live in a deluded state with our perceptions clouded and distorted by greed, anger, and foolishness. Through the practice of Buddhism compassion, wisdom, courage, and hope emerge.

Hope is central to Buddhism. It derives from the confidence that we can fundamentally change for the better and contribute to the improvement of society and the world.

You do not have to participate in an organized religion to have spiritual hope.

If you believe there is a greater force other than our physical being on Earth, you have spiritual hope.

If you can feel a higher spiritual connection with the universe you will never be alone.

A friend measures their satisfaction by your own.

Whether you are drawn to the great traditional religions or decide to follow your own path, making time for your soul can bring great spiritual hope and comfort.

All things shall be well…and all manner of things shall be well.
Julian of Norwich

Beyond your physical self, beyond your thoughts and emotions, there lies a realm within that is pure hope.
From here all things are possible.

          Deepak Chopra

True hope can only be found through the pursuit of something greater than yourself.

Hope is your seeking, hope is your inner urge, hope is your flight up into the Beyond.

Look at all the things in your life that have helped you feel a spiritual connection and try to incorporate them into your daily life.

Fill your home with uplifting music.

Light scented candles and let their gentle aroma infuse your spirit. Think frankincense, myrrh, lavender, and sage.

Color has the power to lift our spirits, soothe our souls, enliven or calm us. Red is for passion, yellow for optimism, orange for security, pink for TLC, blue for calm, and violet for spiritual awareness.

Like breathing air, the spiritual path to hope is fluid, intangible, indefinable, and elusive.

In moments of low hope, spending time quietly communing with nature will help you get in touch with the beauty and wonder that was not created by man.

Watch a spider spinning its web. Listen to a robin singing its song. Savor the smell of newly mown grass.

Greet the sun each morning.

Walk barefoot along the seashore under the stars.

Sit at the water's edge and listen to the lapping waves.

Hear the sound of the trees blowing in the wind.

Close your eyes and
feel some tree bark.

Run barefoot along the grass and feel hope rising through your inner being.

Never pass up a chance to see what the Universe has found for you.

> Deepak Chopra

Cherish your ability to believe and stay true to your beliefs, whatever they are.

Always be ready to stand up to anyone who asks you to account for the hope that is in you, yet do it with a gentleness and reverence.

Unlock the poet inside you.
Draw inspiration from:
- Rabindranath Tagore
- Kahlil Gibran
- Basho Matsuo

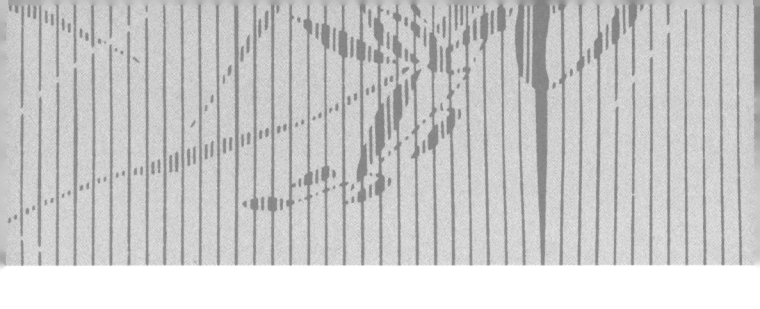

Cultivate harmony and balance in your life with yoga and tai chi.

Hope can come from just being.

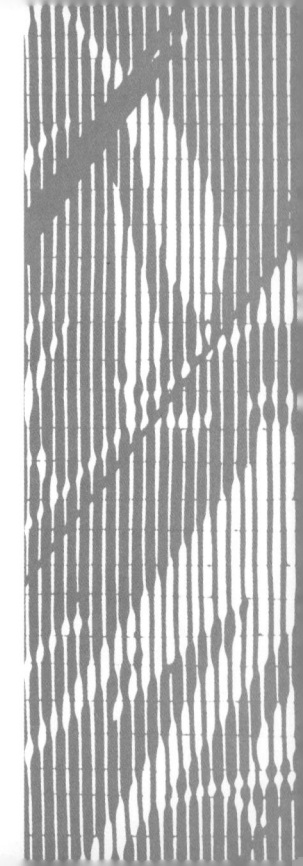

Create a special place in your home where you can just sit and be. Find a quiet spot in your house or garden, put up your feet and do nothing.

Focus on the flame of a lighted candle and practice some meditation.

Developing your own personal rituals on a routine basis can help you to stay connected to your more spiritual side.

Allow yourself to feel. Sometimes hope can come at unexpected times.

If you feel sad,
don't block it;
If you feel happy,
express it;
If you feel anger,
let it out.

Feed your inner soul with beautiful things:
- Exquisite paintings
- Rolling landscapes
- Classical ballet

Let music be the food of hope. Sound creates vibrations that can alter your personal vibration and immediately uplift your spirits.

Music is an easy way to choose the way you want to feel in any given moment. And the more you join in by whistling, singing, or humming, the more quickly you will feel the positive influences.

Start your day by singing in the shower or bath, and feel your spirits soar.

Relaxation and sleep refresh the body and mind, which in turn helps to stock up your hope reserves.

Being quiet and watchful will help to lose the self-absorption that can be so draining, making you miss the small things in life that can give you hope.

Don't assume that things will never change—especially when you are down. They will but it might take time.

Ask for help if things seem bleak. It is not a sign of weakness.

Go over in your mind what you need to do to make your hopes come true.

Your hopes must be consistent with your own inner beliefs for them to be truly successful.

Confront your issues. You may have to forgive your best friend or stop feeling angry with your sister to be spiritually free to pursue your hopes.

To nurture spiritual hope give yourself time to recharge your batteries.

Take a break from your usual routine. This could be a vacation or simply a walk in the open air somewhere green. When you return you will feel new hope.

Never be afraid to walk alone. Solitude is when hope begins to spring.

The world around us is the biggest inspirer of hope.

Go outside whenever you can. Looking at the life cycles that occur as the seasons change can instill a great sense of optimism and hope.

Early morning can be a spiritual time of day. The dew is still on the ground, the peacefulness allows you to hear the birds singing, and other early risers are more likely to smile as they pass you by.

Having faith in people's essential goodness and the consistent effort to cultivate this goodness in ourselves are the two keys to unleashing the great power of hope.

Assemble an emergency feel-good collection that can immediately boost your spirits. Pick out some music, funny DVDs, your food, scents that uplift you, or activities you can do at a moment's notice that make you feel good. As soon as a negative thought enters your mind choose to ignore it and do something positive.

Mindfulness—stopping and becoming aware of the moment and allowing yourself to be exactly as you are—can summon up feelings of hope and joy. It may help you discover what you really want from life.

Take note of what you are thinking at this moment. Is it negative or positive? Do you want this thought to be creating your future? Just notice and be aware.

Take a walk in your mind to your favorite place, be it a park, woods, or beach that you love. Close your eyes and imagine you are there, taking in fresh, uplifting air with every breath.

Look for the hope in your life and your life will automatically become a hopeful experience.

There is no true beginning or end. The beginning is an end and the end a new beginning.

All of us are searching for hope—for the future, for peace, for happiness.

Hope is the destiny of every life.

We are all in the gutter, but some of us are looking at the stars.

Oscar Wilde

Your thoughts have no power other than what you give them.

It is better to follow an impossible dream than to deny yourself the possible growth and development such a journey can provide.

The Hopeful Personality

A hopeful person knows they deserve the best and goes for it.

Hopeful people keep their goals clearly in mind and are always thinking about new ways of reaching them.

Hopeful people are very active in their thinking.

Hopeful people think positively about themselves because they have achieved their hopes in the past and know they can do so again in the future.

Hopeful people welcome challenges and see them as a normal part of everyday life.

If you learn to focus on hope and feel hopeful, that thought process will soon become a habit in itself.

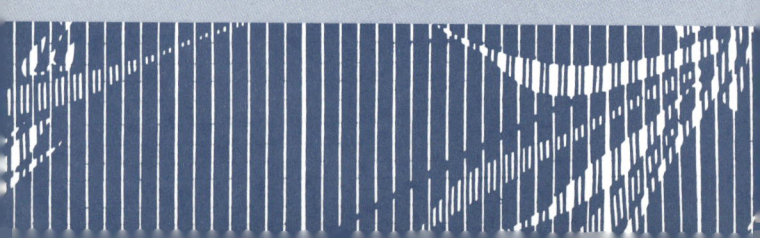

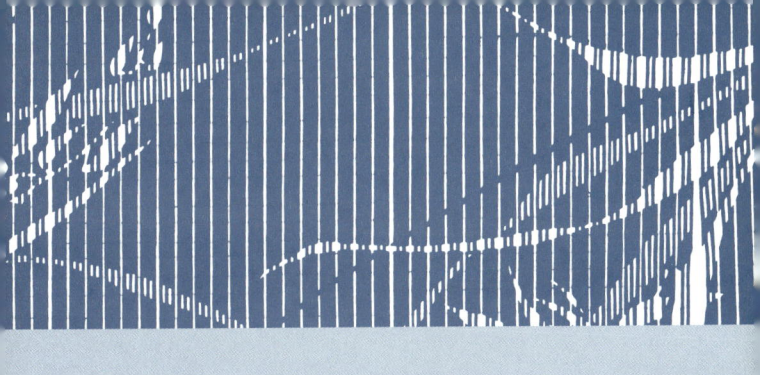

Hopeful people are able to see a broader range of goals than most people.

Hopeful people have better outcomes in their lives than those whose hope levels are on the low side.

The mindset of a hopeful person enables them to stick with it, to have the sense that things, however bad, will pass.

Hopeful people use laughter and fun to get them through the rocky moments.

Hopeful people react positively in the face of stress as they see new pathways around any obstacles to their goals that may arise.

**We are not born with hope.
Hope is a learned way of thinking about yourself.**

Hopeful people use their goals as guides for their journey.

Sometimes you need to be quiet and watchful to develop your hopeful side.

Learn to talk to yourself in a hopeful voice.

Remember you are what you think, you feel what you want.

He who hopes can conquer.

Whatever the mind expects, it finds.

People can sense a hopeful aura and are affected by hopeful thoughts.

Use hopeful words in your inner dialogues.

Smile as much as you can. Smiling encourages hopeful thoughts.

Ignore what others say if you think they could be trying to dash your deepest hopes.

Expecting a positive outcome can increase the likelihood of a hopeful result.

The best of what we are lies in what we hope to be.

No man is brave unless he is afraid.

A troubled mind is not a hopeful mind.

Hope makes the mind more tranquil.

You get to have whatever you choose to hope for.

You have free will to make new choices each and every day.

If you want a hope for life you must think hopeful thoughts.

Having the courage to challenge what we believe to be inevitable enables us to start gathering resources for our journey of hope.

Instead of thinking, "This is hopeless" and "It's not going to get any better," turn your thoughts around to "Where there is hope, there is a way."

Bad things are not the end of the world. Reflecting on hopes can show you there is a solution to most problems.

Try to see beyond your worries and anxiety. They can obstruct the brightest thoughts.

Hopeful thinking can help put setbacks in perspective.

Ask yourself: "How could I view my current situation in a more hopeful light?"

Hopeful people don't bemoan their lot. Instead they try to see the good in every situation.

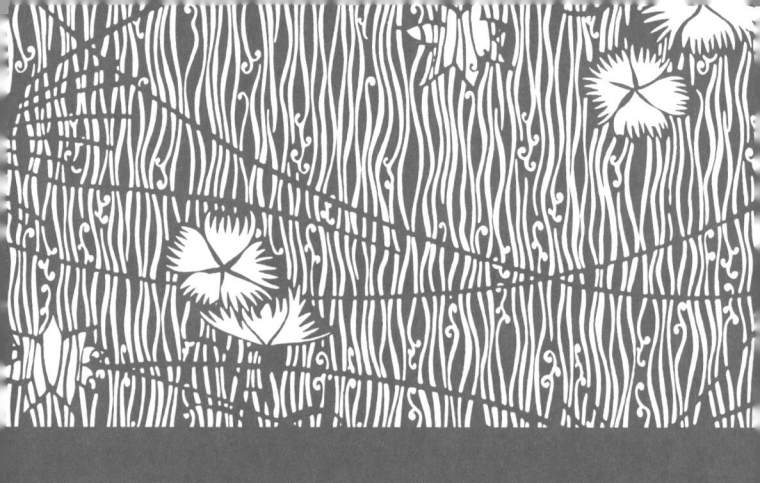

Hopeful people take risks. If you don't take risks you risk stagnation.

Many of the great achievements of life were accomplished by people who went on hoping.

The hopeful person stands strong in the face of any adversity.

If you let yourself think something is hopeless, chances are it will be.

Happy and high-esteem people are those who know what they want from life.

To identify your hopes write a wish list of the important areas of your life, for example, intimate relationships, family, friendships, job, leisure.

Don't put all your hopes in one basket.

Take a tip from high-hope people who spread their hopes across as many areas of their life as possible.

The high-hope way of thinking is to base future hopes on past performance.

Put aside enough time to follow your important hopes.

Make sure you have someone with whom to discuss your hopes.

Affirmative rather than doubting thoughts fire the high-hope person.

Hopeful people persevere in their pursuit of hopes, but are also flexible and can switch their focus when necessary.

People who incorporate hope in their life are more than optimists: they are ready to address problems and act as leaders.

Taking risks and making mistakes are all part of the hopeful process.

New hopes help enliven and invigorate the mind.

Playing positive mental tapes in your head can help keep hopes high.

Patience is part of being hopeful. It may take longer to reach your goals than perhaps you thought when you started out.

High-hope people have positive self-belief that they will get there in the end.

Rather than letting a problem get to you, let your hope get to the problem.

What is hopeful thinking? Thoughts aimed at how to get what you want.

To develop hopeful thinking you need to pay attention to what others around you are thinking. Don't, however, let others dictate your hopes. Instead choose to act deliberately from your own center of calm.

The more hope you have, the more you have to give to others.

A hopeful person surrounds themselves with people, color, sounds, and work that nourish them.

Take the initiative and don't wait for things to happen.

You must first be who you really are, then do what you need to do, in order to get what you hope for.

Learn to say no to anything except the most important priorities in your life. Only then will you have sufficient space for good and positive things to come into your thoughts.

A hopeful person knows that his ambitions, needs, and wants really do matter.

Be aware of your inner wisdom—trust yourself and go with your gut feelings.

Keep a *Book of Hope* in which you write down all the good things that have happened—from the smile of a child to a shaft of sunlight streaming through the window. Use it to stimulate hopeful thoughts when you feel low.

It is up to you whether to fill your mind with hope or not. Choose to and see how it opens an inner well of strength.

Once you have made your choice there will be no going back. A person of hope will always go forward.

Recognize that even if disaster strikes it too will pass and you have the strength of character to survive it. Your hopes will carry you through.

Life changes begin when you start to make changes.

Success is about identifying your hopes and what you feel passionate about and enjoy.

A hopeful person:
- Goes to the gym
- Visits art galleries
- Signs up for an evening course

Hope is not what we are, but what we do and think.

People with hope are the happiest people in the world.

Hopeful people are more extrovert, more sociable, and more agreeable.

Hope is a flame we nurture within our heart. Someone else may spark it but it is up to us to keep it burning.

He who has hope has everything.

Being hopeful is a natural part of the human condition. We just need to believe it and allow ourselves to feel it.

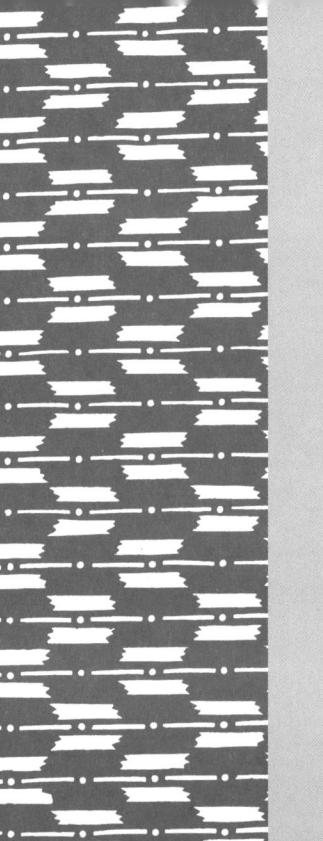

BEACONS OF HOPE:
Diana, Princess of Wales
Mother Teresa
Nelson Mandela
Pope John Paul II

Think about the hopeful people in your life. Analyze what makes them stand out in the crowd, then take a leaf out of their book.

Feeling hopeful is contagious. It uplifts everyone around you and raises the vibration so that your environment reflects your sunny disposition.

Hopeful people have discovered how to enjoy life to the fullest. You can benefit by spending time with them.

The difference between winners and others is that winners make their hopes happen while the rest just let them happen.

Accept accountability for your thoughts, feelings, and actions because they create your future hopes.

THE EIGHT ATTRIBUTES OF HOPEFUL PEOPLE:

1. I can think of many ways to get out of a jam.
2. I energetically pursue my goals.
3. There are lots of ways around any problem.
4. I can think of many ways to get the things in life that are most important to me.
5. Even when others get discouraged, I know I can find a way to solve the problem.
6. My past experiences have prepared me well for my future.
7. I've been pretty successful in life.
8. I meet the goals that I set for myself.

C. R. Snyder

**If you can't feel hope,
it's time to create some.**

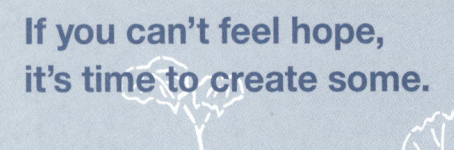

He who hopes
knows that the
bus will come.

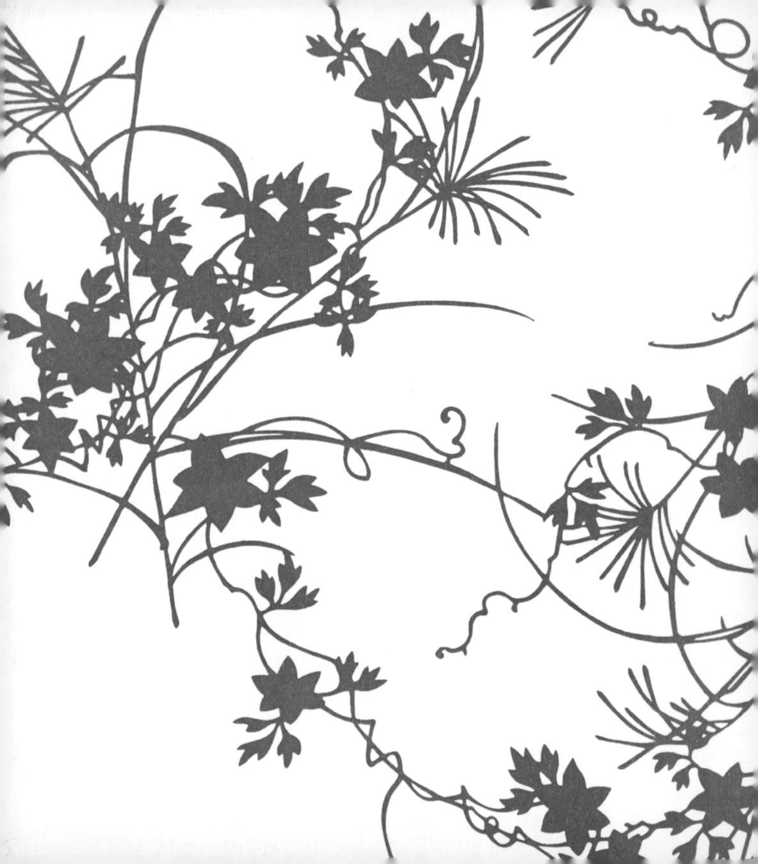

Words of Hope

Take short views, hope for the best, and trust in God.
>Revd Sydney Smith

Only those who will risk going too far can possibly find out how far one can go.
>T. S. Eliot

The thoughts we choose to think are the tools we use to paint the canvas of our lives.

Louise Hay

Through your intent, you can literally command the Laws of Nature to fulfill your dreams and desires.

Deepak Chopra

The best thing about the future is that it only comes one day at a time.

Abraham Lincoln

And the day came when the risk it took to remain tight in a bud was more painful than the risk it took to blossom.

Anaïs Nin

Learn to get in touch with the silence within yourself, and know that everything in this life has purpose. There are no mistakes, no coincidences. All events are blessings given to us to learn from.

    Elizabeth Kubler-Ross

My greatest source of hope…
is the energy, commitment and…courage of young people when they know the problems and are empowered to act. They are changing the world.

Dr. Jane Goodall

In today's world full of agony and pain, we have no choice but to equip ourselves with the patience and hope that will see us to the safest shore of the lake.

Ziyad Alawneh

To lose hope is to lose the capacity for shared imagination; hope is an act that builds and is sustained by community.

W. W. Meissner

Hope of ill gain is the beginning of loss.

                Democritus

Hope is brightest when it dawns from fears.

                Sir Walter Scott

In each of us are places where we have never gone. Only by pressing the limits do you ever find them.

                Joyce Brothers

To hope means to be ready at every moment for that which is not yet born, and yet not become desperate if there is no birth in our lifetime. Those whose hope is weak settle for comfort or for violence, those whose hope is strong see and cherish signs of new life and are ready every moment to help the birth of that which is ready to be born.

Erich Fromm

I am one with the very power that created me and this power has given me the power to create my own circumstances.

Louise Hay

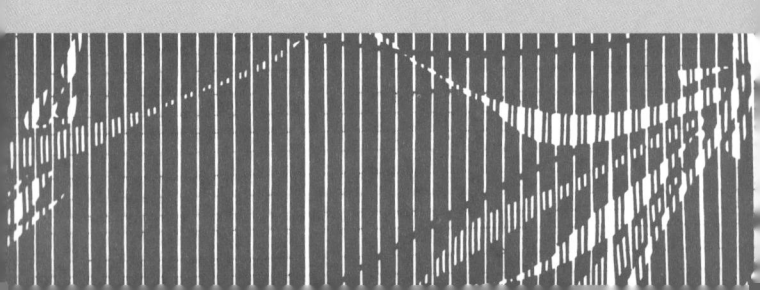

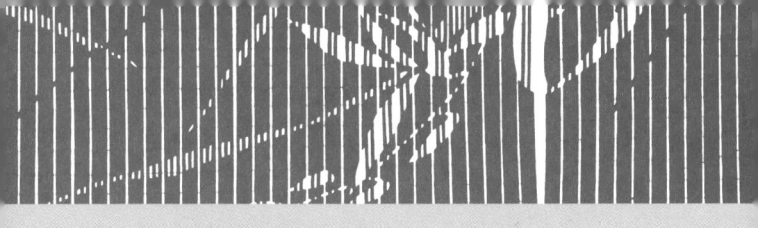

All the interests of [man's] reason, speculative as well as practical, combine in the following three questions: What can I know? What ought I to do? And for what may I hope?

Emmanuel Kant

Hope is an essential vitamin for social processes. If everybody awoke each day to announce "it's hopeless," there would be no plausible tomorrow and no continuous social arrangements.

Lionel Tiger

Life and hope entirely depend on inner wisdom.

       Sri Chinmoy

Life is the car. Hope is the engine. Aspiration is the fuel. God is the Destination.

      Sri Chinmoy

Oh God our help in ages past, our hope for years to come. Our shelter from the stormy blast and our eternal home. There is hope for us all.

Isaac Watts

If life is to be sustained hope must remain, even where confidence is wounded, trust impaired.

Erik Erikson

The young are full of passion which excludes fear and of hope which inspires confidence.

Aristotle

Hope and the freedom to choose are the things which make life worth living. If we have those we can feel that we have a chance of getting everything else that we want.

Dorothy Rowe

Imagination is the highest kite one can fly. Your only obligation in any lifetime is to be true to yourself. Being true to anyone else or anything else is impossible.

Richard Bach

Low-hope children are like small boats lost in the darkness of a threatening sea. A good role model provides a lighthouse of hope for a safe passage.

C. R. Snyder

Each time a man stands up for an ideal or acts to improve the lot of others, or strikes out against injustice, he sends out a ripple of hope, and crossing each other from a million centers of energy and daring, those ripples build a current that can sweep down the mightiest walls of oppression and resistance.

Robert F. Kennedy

It is not what we get but what we become by our endeavours that makes them worthwhile.

John Ruskin

Where would life be if we had no courage to attempt anything?

Vincent Van Gough

God planted hope in the desolated hearts of Eve and Adam. This was not a hope that simply expected God to do something for them
in the future.

Adventist Review

Hope is rooted in God's promises, and His promises always have an impact on the present of human existence.
Adventist Review

If it were not for hope
the heart would break.
Thomas Fuller

What oxygen is to the lungs, such is hope to the meaning of life.
       Emil Brunner

A leader is a dealer in hope.
       Napoleon Bonaparte

**Feed your faith and your
fears will starve to death.**
> Anon

While there's life, there's hope.
> 16th-century proverb

**The warrior of life is a believer.
Because he believes in miracles,
miracles begin to happen.
Because he believes his
thoughts can change his life,
his life begins to change.**
> Paulo Coelho

Hope is a good breakfast, but a bad supper.
  Francis Bacon

Hope springs
eternal in the
human breast:
Man never is,
but always
To be blest.
  Alexander Pope

Land of Hope and Glory: Mother of the Free.

A. C. Benson

Most of what has moved the world onwards began as a hope; all of what has moved it backwards has involved the death of hopes.

A. C. Grayling

To travel hopefully is a better thing than to arrive.
   Robert Louis Stevenson

A second marriage is the triumph of hope over experience.
   Samuel Johnson

He who has never hoped can never despair.
George Bernard Shaw

You must not lose faith in humanity. Humanity is an ocean; if a few drops of the ocean are dirty, the ocean does not become dirty.

Mahatma Gandhi

> The natural flights of the human mind are not from pleasure to pleasure but from hope to hope.
>
> Samuel Johnson

And have hope toward God, which they themselves also allow, that there shall be a resurrection of the dead, both of the just and unjust.

The Bible (Acts 24:16)

Hope is a state of mind, not of the world. Hope, in this deep and powerful sense, is not the same as joy that things are going well, or willingness to invest in enterprises that are obviously heading for success, but rather an ability to work for something because it is good.

Vaclav Havel

> Hope is some extraordinary spiritual grace that God gives us to control our fears, not to oust them.
>
> Vincent McNabb

When by my solitary
hearth I sit,
When no fair dreams
before my "mind's
eye" flit,
And the bare heath
of life presents
no bloom;
Sweet Hope, ethereal
balm upon me shed,
And wave thy silver
pinions o'er my head.

John Keats

Hope is the only bee that makes honey without flowers.
　　　　　Robert Ingersol

In reality, hope is the worst of all evils, because it prolongs man's torments.
　　　　　Friedrich Nietzsche

The miserable have no other medicine
But only hope.
    William Shakespeare

Hope is the thing with feathers
That perches in the soul.
And sings the tune
Without the words,
and never stops at all.
        Emily Dickinson

You've gotta have hope. Without hope life is meaningless. Without hope life is meaning less and less.

Anon

The pessimist sees difficulty in every opportunity. The optimist sees the opportunity in every difficulty.

Winston Churchill

The capacity for hope is the most significant fact of life. It provides human beings with a sense of destination and the energy to get started.

Norman Cousins

Expect to have hope rekindled. Expect your prayers to be answered in wondrous ways. The dry seasons in life do not last. The spring rains will come again.

Sarah Ban Breathnach

Fear less, hope more; eat less, chew more; whine less, breathe more; talk less, say more; hate less, love more; and all good things are yours.

Swedish proverb

He that lives in hope danceth without musick.

George Herbert

Hold your head high, stick your chest out. You can make it. It gets dark sometimes, but morning comes…
Keep hope alive.

Jesse Jackson

Hope begins in the dark, the stubborn hope that if you just show up and try to do the right thing, the dawn will come. You wait and watch and work: you don't give up.

Anne Lamott

Hope is a good thing—maybe the best thing, and no good thing ever dies.
      Stephen King

Hope is a talent like any other.
     Storm Jameson

Hope is a vigorous principle…It sets the head and heart to work, and animates a man to do his utmost.

      Jeremy Collier

Hope…is the companion of power, and the mother of success; for who so hopes has within him the gift of miracles.

      Samuel Smiles

Life without hope is an empty, boring, and useless life. I cannot imagine that I could strive for something if I did not carry hope in me. I am thankful to God for this gift. It is as big as life itself.

Vaclav Havel

If you do not hope,
you will not find what is
beyond your hopes.

St. Clement of Alexandria

**In the depths of winter,
I finally learnt in me there
was an invincible summer.**
     Albert Camus

In the face of uncertainty, there
is nothing wrong with hope.
     Bernie S. Siegel

It is above all by the imagination that
we achieve perception and
compassion and hope.

     Ursula LeGuin

It is the around-the-corner brand of hope that prompts people to action, while the distant hope acts as an opiate.
               Eric Hoffer

Men and women are limited not by the place of their birth, not by the color of their skin, but by the size of their hope.
               John Johnson

My theory has always been, that if we are to dream, the flatteries of hope are as cheap, and pleasanter, than the gloom of despair.

                        Thomas Jefferson

Nothing worth doing is completed in our lifetime; therefore we must be saved by hope.

            Reinhold Niebuhr

Of all the forces that make for a better world, none is so indispensable, none so powerful, as hope. Without hope people are only half alive. With hope they dream and think and work.

Charles Sawyer

Our children are our only hope for the future, but we are their only hope for their present and their future.

Zig Ziglar

Pride is one of the seven deadly sins; but it cannot be the pride of a mother in her children, for that is a compound of two cardinal virtues—faith and hope.

Charles Dickens

There are three things I was born with in this world, and there are three things I will have until the day I die—hope, determination, and song.

Miriam Makeba

We judge of man's wisdom by his hope.

Ralph Waldo Emerson

We must accept finite disappointment, but we must never lose infinite hope.
    Dr. Martin Luther King Jr.

Always direct your thoughts to those truths that will give you confidence, hope, joy, love, thanksgiving, and turn away your mind from those that inspire you with fear, sadness, depression.
    Bertrand Wilbertforce

Everything that is done in the world is done by hope.
    Martin Luther

Great hopes make great men.
>   Thomas Fuller

Hope is itself a species of happiness and, perhaps, the chief happiness which this world affords.
>   **Samuel Johnson**

I am not interested in the past. I am interested in the future, for that is where I expect to spend the rest of my life.
>   Charles F. Kettering

I have learned this at least by my experiment: that if one advances confidently in the direction of his dreams, and endeavours to live the life which he has imagined, he will meet with a success unexpected in common hours.

Henry David Thoreau

If you wish success in life, make perseverance your bosom friend, experience your wise counsellor, caution your elder brother, and hope your guardian genius.

Joseph Addison

I have not the shadow of a doubt that any man or woman can achieve what I have, if he or she would make the same effort and cultivate the same hope and faith.

      Mahatma Gandhi

Today, well lived, makes every yesterday a dream of happiness and every tomorrow a vision of hope.

      Sanskrit proverb

Hope is a waking dream.

      Aristotle

Courage is like love; it must have hope to nourish it.

Napoleon Bonaparte

Man is, properly speaking, based upon hope, he has no other possession but hope; this world of his is emphatically the place of hope.

Thomas Carlyle

There is one thing which gives radiance to everything. It is the idea of something around the corner.

G. K. Chesterton

You assume there is no hope, you guarantee there will be no hope.
          Noam Chomsky

It is difficult to say what is impossible, for the dream of yesterday is the hope of today and the reality of tomorrow.
          Robert Goddard

The work goes on, the cause endures, the hope still lives, and the dreams shall never die.
          Edward Kennedy

Hope has as many lives as a cat or a king.
        Henry Wadsworth Longfellow

Man needs, for his happiness, not only the enjoyment of this or that, but hope and enterprise and change.

       Bertrand Russell

There are certain things that our age needs. It needs, above all, courageous hope and the impulse to creativeness.

       Bertrand Russell

True hope is swift, and flies with swallow's wings;
Kings it makes gods, and meaner creatures kings.

       William Shakespeare

To love, and bear; to hope till hope creates from its own wreck the thing it contemplates.

                          Percy Bysshe Shelley

Man can live about forty days without food, about three days without water, about eight minutes without air, but only for one second without hope.

                                 Joseph Addison

To keep the heart unwrinkled, to be hopeful, kindly, cheerful, reverent— that is to triumph over old age.

                          Thomas Bailey Aldrich

Whoever, in middle age, attempts to realize the wishes and hopes of his early youth, invariably deceives himself. Each ten years of a man's life has its own fortunes, its own hopes, its own desires.

Goethe

Maybe all one can do is hope to end up with the right regrets.

Arthur Miller

Ah, Hope! What would life be, stripped of thy encouraging smiles, that teach us to look behind the dark clouds of today, for the golden beams that are to gild the morrow.

Susanna Moodie

Man needs, for his happiness, not only the enjoyment of this or that, but hope and enterprise and change.

Bertrand Russell

You don't seem to realize that a poor person who is unhappy is in a better position than a rich person who is unhappy. Because the poor person has hope. He thinks money would help.

Jean Kerr

There is no hope of joy except in human relations.

Antoine de Saint-Exupéry

Never give in, never give in, never; never; never; never—in nothing, great or small, large or petty—never give in except to convictions of honour and good sense.

Winston Churchill

Enthusiasm is the yeast that makes your hopes rise to the stars. Enthusiasm is the sparkle in your eyes, the swing in your gait, the grip of your hand, the irresistible surge of will and energy to excite your ideas.

Henry Tor

Keep on going and the chances are you will stumble on something, perhaps when you are least expecting it. I have never heard of anyone stumbling on something sitting down.

Charles F. Kettering

A poor man with nothing in his belly needs hope, illusion, more than bread.

Georges Bernanos

Hope can vanish but can die not.
　　　　Percy Bysshe Shelley

He has no hope who never had a fear.

　　　　　　　William Cowper

**A man awaits his end
Dreading and hoping all.**
　　　　　　　W. B. Yeats

An Hachette Livre UK Company

First published in Great Britain by MQ Publications
a division of Octopus Publishing Group Ltd
2–4 Heron Quays, London, E14 4JP
www.octopusbooks.co.uk

Copyright © Octopus Publishing Group Ltd, 2008
Text © Jane Garton, 2008

Distributed in the United States and Canada by
Hachette Book Group USA
237 Park Avenue
New York
NY 10017

All rights reserved. No part of this publication may used or
reproduced or transmitted in any form or by any means, electronic
or mechanical, including photocopying, recording, or any
information storage and retrieval system now known or to be
invented without permission in writing from the publishers.

Jane Garton, asserts the moral right to be identified as the
author of this book.

ISBN 13 978-1-84601-283-9
ISBN 10 1-84601-283-X

A CIP catalogue record for this book is available from
the British Library.

10 9 8 7 6 5 4 3 2 1

Printed and bound in China